There was a Garden

Meditations and Prayers

by

Eddie Askew

and

Jenny Hawke

Other books by Eddie Askew

*A Silence and a Shouting · Disguises of Love,
Many Voices One Voice · No Strange Land,
Facing the Storm · Breaking the Rules,
Cross Purposes · Slower Than Butterflies,
Music on the Wind · Edge of Daylight (Memoirs),
Talking with Hedgehogs · Unexpected Journeys,
Love is a Wild Bird · Encounters · Chasing the Leaves,
Breaking Through · Dabbling with Ducks,
I've been thinking, Lord · It's me again, Lord*

Other books by Eddie Askew and Jenny Hawke

*Walking into the Light (with Stephanie Bell)
Making a Mark*

Published, edited and distributed by TLM Trading Limited
www.tlmtrading.com

First Published 2011, Reprinted 2012
Text by Eddie Askew and Jenny Hawke
Paintings © A.D. (Eddie) Askew OBE

Design and production by Creative Plus Publishing Ltd,
www.creative-plus.co.uk

Printed and bound in Singapore by Imago

ISBN 978-0-902731-93-6

Cover picture: *Flower Meadow* by Eddie Askew

*Bible verses from the NIV (New International Version)
used by permission of the International Bible Society.*

Contents

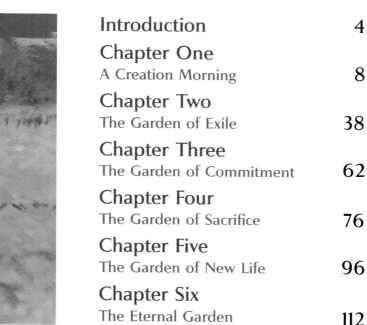

Dedication

This book is dedicated to my wonderful children,
Samuel and Jessamy, who amaze me and bring
me joy, and to my sister, Stephanie, who shared
my childhood and is my dearest friend.

Introduction

This book has been fuelled by three things; love for my father, determination to see it completed, and lots of dark, dark chocolate.

After my father died, I found the unfinished manuscript for *There was a Garden* in his files. I have added my own thoughts, meditations and prayers and completed those chapters that had only been written in note form.

I started out not knowing how it would end. I have travelled with him through the gardens, seeing with his eyes, and with my own. I have learnt as I have written, moved at times to tears by the love of our God, through stories of war, exile, love and betrayal. God remains through it all: loving and merciful, a God interested in each one of our own stories, in all of our personal histories. He redeems things we believe are lost to us forever. He restores faith and hope in spite of outward circumstance.

And he walks with us through the garden of our own lives.

'For there is none like Thee. Oh Lord'

Jenny Hawke

Jenny Hawke, 2011

Throughout the book you'll find my father, Eddie's, writing in black and my contributions in blue, while the pages that we have jointly written appear on a cream tint.

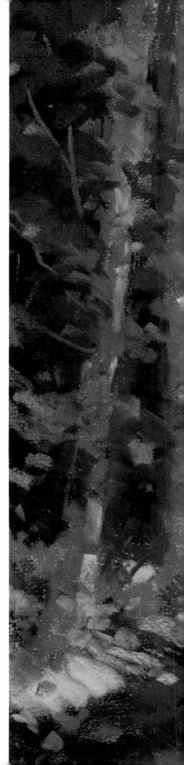

Imagine

Remember a garden where you've been happy, perhaps your own garden or another. Think about it. Imagine being there with a companion, someone you love. Let their presence in your memory bring joy and comfort. Sit together in silence and picture the garden in your mind. The lawn, the hedges, the flower beds and shrubs, the colours. Enjoy it.

Now think of your ideal garden. Would it be a formal garden, neat well-defined paths with clipped box hedges? Well-tended flower beds with everything in its place and given room to grow, the lawn well-trimmed. No weeds.

Perhaps you see a cottage garden with a profusion of flowers given the freedom to grow and blossom as they will, the lawn well used by family and pets. Toys scattered across it. A swing. A sundial.

Maybe your dream is a walled garden, quiet, secure, sheltered and protected by its warm, high brick walls. A garden at peace. Fruit trees spread along the south-facing wall, rambling roses, pink and yellow and white. A large vegetable plot, a well-used greenhouse with an established grape vine.

Could your ideal garden be an orchard, a line of apple trees, their trunks disappearing in the long grass, and a profusion of wild daisies and dandelions and buttercups? At the end a small stream, lined with water plants.

Now, stand for a moment and look around. Feel the sun on your back, warm and comforting. The breeze, just strong enough to ruffle your hair. Feel the grass under your feet, or the crunch of the gravel on the path. Listen to the blackbirds, watch the restless sparrows, smell the perfume of the roses. What else do you see, hear, feel, smell? Are you alone with your thoughts, or do you feel a presence, warm as the sun, soft as the breeze? Is someone walking with you in the garden?

One

A Creation Morning

Reading: Genesis

In the beginning God created the heavens and the earth.
Genesis 1:1

Then God said, "Let us make man in our image, in our likeness, and let them rule over the fish of the sea and the birds of the air, over the livestock, over all the earth, and over all the creatures that move along the ground." So God created man in his own image, in the image of God he created him; male and female he created them.
Genesis 1:26–27

Now the LORD God had planted a garden in the east, in Eden; and there he put the man he had formed. And the LORD God made all kinds of trees grow out of the ground– trees that were pleasing to the eye and good for food. In the middle of the garden were the tree of life and the tree of the knowledge of good and evil.
Genesis 2:8–9

In the beginning...
Genesis 1:1

It was still dark when I got up. I struggled out of my sleeping bag, opened the rickety wooden door and stepped out into the cold. There was a fresh coating of frost over everything, and yesterday's puddles were frozen hard. The air was still, crystal clear, almost tangible. I felt that a sudden movement might shatter it like glass. We were high in the Himalayas, in the mountains of Bhutan. In the dusk of the day before, we had come over the pass at 14,500 feet, and spent the night a little lower down in a small government guest house.

As I watched, the sun peeked on tiptoe over the dark mountain ridge in front of me, throwing long shadows across the rough ground. The light first touched the hills behind me, slowly sliding honey-gold down the slopes to the cloud layer in the valley, sweeping the darkness away in front of it.

Then I caught some of the sounds of silence, those small natural noises our ears so often filter out. The sound of nearby water running down over rocks, melting frost, dripping dewdrops on the ground, the crunch of dry snow underfoot. Then a bird called, hidden but beautiful and full of morning optimism. A distant dog barked and then another answered, and after a pause, far away, a human voice echoed across the valley.

It was a creation morning. I had watched light forming out of darkness, seen sunshine gather itself, heard the sounds of life in melting ice and water, bird and beast and human voice. Later, as the sun rose higher and its rays probed deeper, the cloud layer below thinned and dissolved, and in the warmth, life began to move a little faster, the colours of the landscape strengthening, brightening.

There was an innocence and purity about the morning, the day just beginning, an innocence so easily lost. Creation is not simply a once-and-for-all event, but a daily renewal; the hand of God reshaping, reforming, reinvigorating his world. Each day repeats, until the end of time, the reassurance of his power, and the renewal of the promise of his presence and energy in the world. An offer made in love, at once cosmic and personal, warming and dependable like nothing else.

Then I was called into breakfast. It was only bread and fruit, but it tasted like loaves and fishes.

Meditation

An ordinary dawn.
Velvet black gives way to gold.
Majesty of mountain
and frosted dew.
Birdsong answers across deep valley
and calls the morning
into being.
Soft noise as sleep is rubbed away
and purpose moves both man and beast.

And yet this ordinary dawn
the miracle repeats.
Night follows day
and day follows night.
Creation wakes
and the possibility begins
again
of finding your love
in every living thing.

Prayer

Lord, in the light of the morning,
its colour
beauty
and joy,
I see your constancy.

In the dusty heat of midday,
when light shimmers
and the world is still,
I see your constancy.

In the rhythm of the seasons,
through rain and snow,
sun and shade,
I know your constancy.

Your hand
reshaping,
reforming,
reinvigorating my world.
Each day different,
brings an optimism each morning.

I commit this day to you.
You give me the freedom
to make of it what I will.
Your constancy,
and your love for me
are all I need
today.

Thank you, Lord.

The Glory of the Universe

In the beginning...
Genesis 1:1

In the beginning of what? The beginning of our planet, Earth. A planet tiny in the immensity of creation? Surely we're talking bigger than that? Let's include the sun, moon, stars – more stars than the wise men could have dreamed of. So are we just talking of our galaxy then? But the astronomers tell us there are thousands of galaxies, millions of stars beyond our sight, many known only by the effect of their gravity on other stars. Galaxies unknown to us, but known to God. Beyond our imagination, but not beyond his concern and creativity. Our minds struggle to expand, to keep up with the glory of the expanding universe. A question we can never answer. Simply hold on to God's presence and his energy that assures us of sunrise and sunset for as long as he wills it.

I was walking the dog. It was late on a winter evening, the air still and crisp. No clouds, and frost forecast for later. The moon was full, the stars bright in the night sky. I paused, looked up and around. It was one of those rare 'thin' moments when my ordinary, prosaic life was suddenly penetrated by the spiritual. I felt buoyed up by the beauty of it all, humbled – yes, really – by the insignificance of my speck of life in the immensity of God's creation. And small though I felt, overwhelmed by the conviction, the certainty, that God loved me, unconditionally.

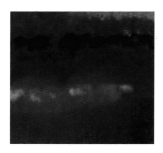

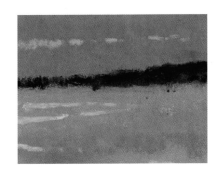

Meditation

The night sky, Lord,
immense indigo blue,
stretches over me.
Unfathomable dimensions,
like the depth of your love.

Tremulous light
from named and un-named stars,
yet you know them all.
I imagine the imprint of your hand
on each one,
Creator God.

And as I stand,
alone in the half-light,
the earth beneath
moves in silent orbit.
Set in space
by invisible force,
guided and held
in constant dance.

I stand in awe.
Mystery so great,
so wonderful.
My questions remain,
cradled by your love.
And I am still
beneath and before you.

Prayer

Lord, let me never lose this child-like wonder
at your astonishing world.
Your gift to me,
to us,
to be surrounded always
by star upon star,
by the constant change of sea and sky,
by leaf-fall and blessed new growth,
by fluted birdsong as day fades to dusk.

Thank you for your creation,
a constant joy,
and a reminder of your love
and your greater plan for us all.
I am so grateful.

What Sort of God?

In the beginning, God...
Genesis 1:1

And what sort of God? We build our own picture of him – or her – through our experience of life. To some, God is a threatening and demanding personality, who is deeply disturbed by human frailty and reacts against it. To others, he is the God of Love, perfect love – and if his love is perfect, I can't believe him to be angry and judgmental one day and loving the next. A God – the God – of perfect love is always loving. Otherwise there is no logic to it. Is God logical? Mathematicians think so; God the perfect equation. To me he is the artist creator, one who can move effortlessly from broad brush stroke to intimate detail in an instant, one for whom nothing is too great or too small.

"The whole world," says Virginia Woolf, "is a work of art."

It is not a two-dimensional painting, inspired though that can be, nor even a sculpture in three dimensions, beautiful yet limited to a particular space, but a creation that is constantly changing, enlarging, dying and renewing; a great awe-inspiring drama of life. God throws the whole of his energy and personality into the act of creation and loves with an infinite love everything that he has created.

We would expect no less from a God who has neither beginning nor end. If he had he wouldn't be God; he'd be finite like the rest of us. Creation is no accident, no random gathering of atoms and energy, it's a gift. Creation is a gift of grace from a God who gives freely and generously. And who continues to do so for he's not only creator but also sustainer, and ultimately, redeemer.

The more we humans explore and push out the boundaries of what we know about our tiny part of the cosmos, the greater, not less, the wonder and mystery grows. Mystery grows with knowledge. The more we learn, the more we realise how little we really know, and the more incredible seems the idea that it's all accidental. Our creation is part of God's purposes, our life his gift, the breath of God himself.

Meditation

It's so easy
to miss the joy of Creation,
in the grey of an ordinary day.
We have 'things to do',
and lists to complete.
There seems no space
to look up and see
with the eyes of a child
and revel in the mystery
of the 'why?'

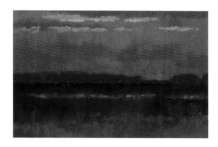

Prayer

Lord,
sometimes it seems the more I know
the less I understand of you.
New discovery leads me to more uncertainty.
The universe expands
and so, it seems, do my doubts.
Yet their potency fades
in the depth of your love.
Your grace surrounds me.

Lord,
when I feel small
and sometimes of little worth,
help me realise
that I too am a precious part
of your unfolding creation.

Thank you.

The Beginning of Faith

In the beginning, God created...
Genesis 1:1

The first words of the Bible. That is exactly where faith begins. One uncompromising statement of our origin. It doesn't matter so much what comes next. That is the essence. Something many people find difficult to accept, but believers of all faiths base everything else on it. Before creation, before anything else was, other than chaos, God was alive and well and totally beyond our understanding. Which he still is.

God has no beginning and no end. If he had, he wouldn't be God. He'd be finite like the rest of us.

'In the beginning God...' That's the starting point for everyone. "Hands that flung stars into space," as Graham Kendrick, the hymn-writer, so movingly puts it. A belief that there's a purpose behind creation, a purpose behind the 'coming into being' – that's what *genesis* means – and a power that sustains and renews its energy. And while God can't be proved objectively, he is proved again and again in the lives of all who take his authorship of creation on board. Rejecting God doesn't get rid of God. The most militant atheists simply create an alternative faith–system for themselves because within this world, for them, God doesn't exist.

In the beginning God created...

God has no beginning and no end because he exists out of time. We're told that God promised eternal life 'before the beginning of time' (*Titus 1:2*), and time was his creation.

And if God existed out of human time before the Earth's creation, then I can't really see why we use so much energy disagreeing with each other over the actual length of time of a Genesis-day. I'm not really worried about whether God created our world in six 24-hour days or billions of years. For it was through his wisdom and love that he created our universe and he decided that 'it was very good'. Nothing can take away the complexity, the power and the grandeur of God in his work of creation.

Time may exist for us in measurable quantities – notably my alarm clock – but not for God. I suggest the psalmist has it right when he sings, 'for a thousand years in your sight are like a day that has just gone by, or like a watch in the night' (*Psalm 90:4*). And Peter reminds us, 'With the Lord a day is like a thousand years, and a thousand years are like a day' (*2 Peter 3:8*).

This perhaps explains why God is so patient with us and our little arguments, although I reckon he'd be much happier if we occupied our time in healing the sick and comforting those who mourn, rather than quarreling with each other. The writer Jonathan Swift, who also became the Dean of St Patrick's Cathedral in Dublin said, "We have enough religion to hate one another, but not enough to love one another" (*Gulliver's Travels,* Jonathan Swift, 1726). I guess that's the difference between 'religion' and real faith. In the beginning God... Let's live every day in the light of these words, aware of his continuing creation around us and in us.

Blossoming

The mystery remains
and I am glad.
Let's keep some secrets
from the scientists
and all who would reduce life
to mechanics.
Beyond
the weighing
and the measuring
and the theorising,
I know only one thing
with certainty:
once I was dead
but now I am alive.

Prayer

Lord,
let me remember,
when theology
threatens to divide
and cloud my
understanding,
your truth remains.

Your gospel is love.

And because of you,
I have life,
God-breathed,
eternal,
and freely given.

God's Good Garden

*Now the Lord God planted
a garden in the east, in Eden.*
Genesis 2:8

I live in a village. It's an ancient village, near a ford on the River Trent, used by Stone Age people. The remains of a Roman villa have been found nearby. The Romans loved gardens and so do I. In my case, not so much to work in, I must admit, more to relax and enjoy. Eight hundred years before the Romans, the Babylonians gardened, and a thousand years after the Romans, the Persians were still gardening.

When I take the dog for a walk, I look at the gardens we pass. The dog appreciates gardens too, but she has a different agenda so I keep her on the lead. One road is all bungalows. They're built to a pattern, all very much the same, but not so the front gardens. It's through the gardens that folk express themselves.

Some are highly disciplined with neat, square lawns, always trimmed. The bedding plants – red geraniums and blue lobelia are spaced out precisely. Then there are slightly untidy gardens, odd weeds and dandelions growing where they shouldn't. In between a few low-maintenance gardens totally paved over or gravelled, with a few shrubs and a rock as a focal point. And just a couple of gardens with high hedges that block my view. I try to guess what each one suggests about the gardener's personality, but we'll leave that thought there.

Now God planted a garden...
I note the verb – planted, not made. I think there is a difference. 'Made' suggests a finished product, complete and final in its moment of creation. 'Planted' tells us that God's garden was alive. Gardens are living organisms that develop, change and grow. My lawn and a vigorous hawthorn hedge tell me that.

The way a garden looks today is not the same as it looked a year ago. In autumn it will look radically different from how it looked in spring. And in the cold of winter, different again. It may look dark and brooding and dead, but it's filled with promise. Bulbs germinate, grow, blossom and appear to die only to find new life again.

Our relationship with God is organic, a living experience and therefore full of change. My experience of God today is different – hopefully deeper although I'm not the one to judge that – from what it was 20 years ago, and it's important to give the experience space to grow, to find the nourishment its roots need to strengthen their hold on him. To set our experience of God in a time warp where nothing is allowed to change, where any new thought or variation is strongly resisted, may result in loss.

I am sad when I see a Christian group that allows nothing to change, which permits no new understanding to penetrate the rigidity of its beliefs. Such a group is sterile. It is dying without realising it. God is constantly calling us on to journey with him, waiting and eager to reveal new depths of his love to us. R.S. Thomas, that passionate Welsh Christian poet, wrote that we only see God's back. He is always one step ahead, calling us to follow.

Gardens are never finished, never complete. Enthusiastic gardeners say there is always room for another plant. And there is always more work to do. We need to keep ourselves open to the hand of God still hoeing in our lives. And open to his gentle pruning.

Meditation

A single tiny seed,
planted alone
in the waiting darkness
of good soft earth.
With promise of gentle rain
and warmth of sun to come,
the miracle begins.
The seed shifts within.
Energy that created cosmos and life
itself
pushes root
down and down,
twisting this way and that,
taking hold
and multiplying its long length.

It shifts again,
and fragile shoot finding sweet air
turns to face the Sun
with welcome recognition.

Prayer

Lord,
remind me from time to time,
that my relationship with you
is dynamic,
a living thing.
It needs to grow,
to develop,
to push its roots down deeper
into the quietness and depth
of your love for me.
To stretch its branches towards the
sun,
to yield its fruit in season
to withstand the heat of the day.
"Planted by streams of water,"
you say.
Your living water,
that never fails,
always refreshing.
A cooling balm
to my sometimes weary spirit.

Remind me, Lord,
and nourish me with your love,
again,
today.

A Thing of Beauty

And the Lord God made all kinds of trees
to grow out of the ground – trees that were
pleasing to the eye and good for food.
Genesis 2:9

Driving in India from Delhi to Agra along the Grand Trunk Road is a
fascinating, often nerve-wracking, experience. It is a chaos of exotically
decorated and heavily overloaded commercial trucks, government jeeps,
and crowded taxis impatiently trying to overtake everything else. Down the
road's centre, myopic motorcyclists weave, and ignoring everything else, pass
slow-moving farm carts pulled by bullocks and, occasionally, camels. The
road is lined with trees. Ugly trees. Trees that have been hacked and slashed,
their wonderful branches reduced to tortured stumps, the result of human
desperation. Driven by poverty, people scavenge for fuel to cook their food.
Young boys tear down leaves to feed their goats and herds of cattle. Some
trees die completely, others manage somehow to survive, writhing in silent
agony. Not the way it was meant to be.

God is an artist. He made, and still makes, trees pleasing to the eye. I can't think of any tree in its natural state that isn't pleasing to the eye. Each has a grace, a presence that speaks of God's creation. And during a European autumn and winter, they lose their leaves and we are confronted with the bare grace of trunk and branch beneath.

God was creating beauty right from the start. The next verse, Genesis 2:10, follows with 'a river watering the garden'. Trees and water. What more could a painter want? God's will was to fill our lives with beauty and delight. Eden means a place of delight, a paradise we say; and 'paradise' is a Persian word meaning a pleasure garden. Some commentators point out that even in pleasure gardens, the gardeners have to work, but most gardeners say they enjoy working in their gardens.

Taj. St. Valentine's Day 2001

Later, as you arrive in Agra, nerves frayed from the four-hour journey, you reach the entrance to the Taj Mahal. And written in Arabic script over the entrance of the gate is written 'If there is a paradise on earth it is here, it is here, it is here.'

God's purpose for humankind was that they were to be planted in the garden, to grow in the beauty and delight that flows from the presence of God. It was God's garden – we read of him taking his evening walk in it, a lovely image – did he dead-head the roses as he walked or were there no dead flowers in Eden?– and humanity was meant to share it. In the garden where God is, where his presence is real and tangible, there is paradise.

"He who is filled with love, is filled with God," said St Augustine.

The garden was to be a place of innocence and pure joy in his presence. And the psalmist gives us a faint echo of the reality that those who are 'right' with God are nourished and given all they need to grow to their full potential, 'like a tree planted by streams of water' (*Psalm 1:3*).

Meditation

An evening walk with you, Lord?
What would I say?
How would it feel
to walk by your side,
to feel the warmth of your breath,
to match my step with yours?

And as we walk,
beauty and fragrance surround,
the light of your presence
showing the way ahead,
the path smooth to my feet.
My heartbeat slows,
the rush of my world falls away
and I relax
into your acceptance of who I am.

And yet I long to be more for you.
Stronger,
more faithful,
and courageous.
Taking giant steps,
doing great things,
all in your Name.

But all you are asking
is that I walk with you
today.

Prayer

Lord, the world you gave us,
a place of delight
fashioned for us alone.
Lord, we thank you.

All we ever needed,
you placed within the Garden.
Strong leaf and shade,
cool water at our feet.
Every fruit and plant for our use.
Lord, we thank you.

Lord, forgive us our misuse,
when greed replaces care
and your delicate balance is
overturned.
Complex structure falling into chaos
without you.
Lord, forgive us.

Lord, help us to restore
the beauty and the balance
of your gift to us.

Made in his Image

So God created man, humankind, in his own image, in the image of God he created him; male and female, he created them.
Genesis 1:27

Made in the image of God. What does that mean? Not just in the abstract but for us, you and me, all of us, created in the image of God and sharing a common humanity. It means there is something of God in each one of us. That something of his nature, her nature – however you experience God – is there, deep down, part of our essential being. Mother Teresa said that when she looked at anyone, a desperately ill beggar in Kolkata (Calcutta), anyone in great need, she saw Jesus in them. Whatever their wretchedness, however unsavory their appearance, God's likeness is there in every human being. It may lie hidden; it may be struggling to get out from under the deep layers of suffering and neglect. It is part of our essence. In every cell, chromosome, gene. 'We are God's workmanship,' writes St Paul.

Peter Price in *The Undersong* says "spirituality is about the whole of our lives, the ordinary and the extraordinary, the public and the private." In fact the presence of God in our lives makes the ordinary extraordinary and the extraordinary the ordinary. "God is closer to us than we are to ourselves," said St Augustine.

This intimacy of God within us, as an insuperable part of our being, is an awe-inspiring truth that can change everything about our understanding of life. We should never underestimate the value of our life or any human life. It's God's gift and it gives dignity and a value beyond anything. We can stand upright, not just physically, but in the way we see ourselves.

Whatever our circumstances each one of us is special – not in the sense of a supermarket offer, which tends to mean they are trying hard to sell something that's not moving very fast – but special in God's eyes. We are God's works of art and we are called to value ourselves and others. Some of us may be more Picasso than Rembrandt, but God frames us in glory and has a purpose for each one of us.

And that suggests something about the way we see and treat other people. When we ill-treat or ignore others we are in danger of abusing God's image in them. When I see pictures of refugees in Rwanda or Afghanistan, or people with untreated leprosy, it's the loss of dignity that affects me most.

And I suggest we need to react not only with practical compassion, but with anger at what we do to one another. After all the word 'compassion' means 'with passion' and 'passion' originally meant 'entering into the suffering' of someone else. Our creation in God's image tells us that there's a unity to all humankind. There are no second-class citizens in the kingdom of God.

And being in God's image, we are also born with a capacity for love and the need for love. Born for relationship. Love is the heart of God and that is what he transplants into the soil of our lives. And his love in our lives seeks to generate love in return.

St Augustine said, "He who is filled with love is filled with God himself." Jesus crystallized the whole issue when he was asked about the greatest commandment. "Love," he said. "Love the Lord your God with all your heart, soul, mind and strength... and your neighbour as yourself." (*Mark 12:30–31*) Love God, neighbour and self. The three are woven together without a join, like the seamless robe Jesus wore. They can't be pulled apart. The thing that God desires most from us isn't necessarily obedience, it's love. That we should love him as he loves us.

Love can get overgrown and weedy in the communal garden of our world today. Love can be debased and distorted, but the yearning to be loved and to love is alive in us all.

Meditation

Matchless
and incomparable,
exceptional,
extraordinary,
that is what we are.
Created by power beyond knowing,
unique and singular.

None of us the same,
with potential for greatness,
for loving above and beyond,
for dreams and visions,
God-given and God-fuelled.

And your creation goes on
in us and through us.
Spirit-led
image-bearers
of the God of space and time.

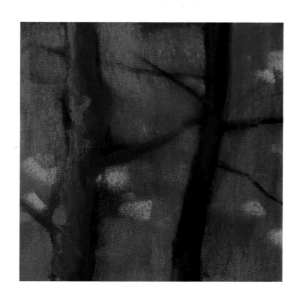

Prayer

Lord,
how can it be?
Made in your image?
When I look in the mirror,
staring back at me,
my face,
imperfect,
tired,
sometimes hopeful,
more often sadly aware of my failings.

In my reflection,
I see my history,
a salt-and-pepper mix
of regrets and achievements.

I've done my best,
or at least I hope so,
but I'd like a re-run,
a chance to do better.

And yet,
you see the real me,
the one you created,
the innocent child within,
full of joy
and playful enthusiasm.

And your love,
immense,
accepting,
and joyous,
overwhelms and humbles me.
Brings me to my knees
and helps me start again,
loving, caring,
and learning to find you
in everyone I see.

Thank you.

The Freedom of God

Then God said, "Let us make man
in our image, in our likeness..."
Genesis 1:26

She was walking through the local shopping area, and she was very pregnant. "Late twenties", I thought. She walked with pride, a look of joy and satisfaction on her face. I looked too, and marvelled, and quietly blessed her. Surely, above everything else this is the greatest, most sacred and wonderful act of creation that human beings are capable of. Co-operating with God in the planting of new life. My interest followed her. I wondered what the future would offer her and her partner, and the child. Would it be a girl or a boy? How would they cope? Where would they all be in 30 years' time?

Next Sunday morning was the Sunday of the month on which our church holds an all-age service. We're fairly relaxed about children in any of our services and the children feel at home. During worship one little girl, about three years old, was on the floor in the aisle. She had a basket of felt-tip pens and several sheets of blank A4 paper. The paper wasn't blank for long. She was oblivious to everything around her and I, as an artist, was equally interested in her work.

It was best classified abstract – which was a polite way of saying scribble. Suddenly she decided it was finished. She sat back on her heels, looked around and picked up her work of art. Holding it in both hands and smiling, she turned to Mummy and showed her. It may have been scribble to me, but it was her creation. She had made her marks. Using that bit of creativity that God had planted in her at birth. And as God saw her painting I reckon he smiled too.

Humankind made in the image of God, in his likeness. To me that means we share in his creativity in everything we do, the large and the small. In forming new life and in the mark-making of tiny children. God wants us to use our freedom and our creativity. He wants us to use our minds. Some Christians leave their minds outside the church door. They stop thinking and are afraid of questioning. God can survive all our questions. The important thing is that we use them in love.

And whether it's in our capacity for love, or our creativity, God gives us freedom. We are not totally determined by our genes and body chemistry, our lives are not totally decided by our upbringing. God gives us freedom to choose our own path, make our own way, and develop our own relationships. And freedom is perhaps the greatest blessing and the greatest danger that humans face.

Meditation

Small beginnings.
A child at play,
immersed in her own creation of line and colour,
absorbed and content, her mother nearby,
repeats the age-old process of joyful imagination.

Prayer

Lord of my beginnings,
small or large,
be Lord of them all.

You give me a blank page
and encourage me to begin,
to colour and draw,
and make my mark,
in the direction I choose.

Lord as I begin this day
with joy,
stay close and guide my hand,
inspiring me to make a
difference.
Let me revel in the colour
and movement on the page.
And whatever mark I make,
let me make it with you in mind.

Reflections: Jenny Hawke

33

Freedom to Love and Be Loved

So God created man in his own image...
Genesis 1:27

Our imagination and our creativity work together. We can use them for good or ill. We design wonderful machines that show us more of the immensity and complexity and beauty of the cosmos and then say God does not exist. "I didn't see him," said the first Russian astronaut in space. He had – he just didn't recognise his presence.

We split the atom and make weapons. We create explosives that can move mountains and we use them in bombs. God created man in his own image. We turn it around to become "Man created God in his own image." We too have taken a bite of the apple; we have listened to the serpent of our own pride. "You will be like God", he said in Genesis 3:5. The freedom to create also contains the seed of the freedom to destroy, the freedom to love and serve includes the freedom to hate and kill. That is the joy and danger of being human.

But for our love towards God to be real there also has to be the freedom to refuse to love God. 'Love is the child of freedom, never that of domination,' said Eric Fromme in *The Art of Loving*. It is through free choice that we step freely over the boundaries God has set in love. Innocence has been destroyed and we are banished from the Garden. I'm not sure about the word 'banished'. It suggests a complete and final cutting off. As though having been driven out we are abandoned. We're not. The image of God is still alive. Damaged but not destroyed. Struggling to make its voice heard. Never taken away from us, and we are never banished from God's presence. That is unthinkable.

We hear echoes of God's spirit in Eden asking "Where are you?" even today. He wants us back. Outside the garden he may not seem so near and intimate but we can still sense a presence. We have a dream, a memory deep within us of the lost garden and a longing to return, to recover the joy and peace and beauty of it. We try to recreate it in our art, music, and poetry. And, in a way, we do it in the gardens around our home. An urge in our finite lives for a glimpse, a feel of the infinite.

And we have a guide. In a 15th-century morality play, *Everyman*, Jesus says, "Everyman, I will go with thee and be thy guide, in thy most need to go by thy side."* In our pilgrimage through the world, God is with us in Jesus. 'Emmanuel – God with us.' He is not the other side of a locked gate, but with us now pointing the way back. The story of the garden isn't only about our origin, but it is also about our destination. God gives us a second chance in Jesus. The place to which we are invited to return, the end of our journey. The garden gate is open, like the open door of the empty tomb, and the Father waits to welcome us home.

*Everyman, *author unknown, 15th-century morality play; quote from the character Knowledge.*

Meditation

An open gate.
A garden beyond.
Something stirs in my memory,
a familiar place. I thought it lost.

And beyond,
an echo,
sometimes soft,
sometimes strong.
Your voice,
calling me by name.

And as I step towards you,
I feel again
the love you have for me,
the immense and overwhelming sense
of acceptance.
unconditional,
beyond my understanding.

I am home,
again,
with you.

Prayer

Show me the way, Lord,
for all my todays
and my tomorrows.
My future's uncertain.
I'd rather know where I'm going.
I'd like to be prepared
for what is to come.
But then again,
maybe it's better this way.
I don't always like change.

But you have set my boundaries.
'The lines have fallen in pleasant places'*
you say,
giving me space to safely grow
into all that you have for me.
Help me to look ahead,
always looking for your footprints,
knowing that you are leading me home.

* Psalm 16:6

37

Two

The Garden of Exile

Reading: 2 Kings 24:10–14

At that time the officers of Nebuchadnezzar king of Babylon advanced on Jerusalem and laid siege to it, and Nebuchadnezzar himself came up to the city while his officers were besieging it. Jehoiachin king of Judah, his mother, his attendants, his nobles and his officials all surrendered to him.

In the eighth year of the reign of the king of Babylon, he took Jehoiachin prisoner. As the LORD had declared, Nebuchadnezzar removed all the treasures from the temple of the LORD and from the royal palace, and took away all the gold articles that Solomon king of Israel had made for the temple of the LORD. He carried into exile all Jerusalem: all the officers and fighting men, and all the craftsmen and artisans—a total of ten thousand. Only the poorest people of the land were left.

Imagine

*The walls of Jerusalem are crowded with armed men. The city is besieged,
surrounded by the army of Nebuchadnezzar, the great king of Babylon – the
most powerful empire of the world. There's a great clash of arms. Jerusalem –
Jerushalom the city of peace, the city of the Great King – is at war. The roar
of battle, the air filled with the sound of war cries and screams of pain. The
beauty and serenity of Eden, the unspoiled earth that God created long gone.
A distant memory. Now the world is a troubled place and people are caught up
in the struggle for power, not for righteousness.*

*The people of Judah can't resist forever and Jerusalem falls. King Jehoiachin,
his family, all the nobility are taken captive to Babylon. The Temple, God's
home was desecrated, looted of all its sacred treasures. Gold, silver, jewels.
Many people were taken into exile, the army, the craftsmen, the metal workers,
the artists, the musicians, the useful and the strong.*

*"Only the poorest people of the land were left," says verse 14. Unwanted even
by the conquering army, they were seen as having no real value or use. Were
they glad to be left behind? I wonder. Some of them must have had some spirit
left because ten years later they rebelled. And again Nebuchadnezzar came
down and this time Jerusalem was totally destroyed and the Temple was burned.
Those who had not been taken away into exile the first time were taken now.*

Exile in Babylon

He carried into exile all Jerusalem
2 Kings 24:14

I was watching a television journalist reporting live (come to think of it, how else can he report?) from one of the many contemporary war zones around the world. Wearing his flak jacket, clutching his microphone and crouching near the ground, his voice was almost drowned out by the noise around him, the crump of mortar shells exploding and the staccato note of automatic weapons.

Listening to it all, I realised that, compared with today's battles, ancient conflicts were far less noisy. The war cries, the frightened and anguished screams of terribly injured men, the terror of innocent women and children were all the same, as the army of the king of Babylon was struggling to capture Jerusalem, but there were no explosives or gunfire.

And then came the process of exile, being forced to leave everything familiar and face the unknown. Come back to the present. Look around your home, your house or flat, your favourite room and ask yourself if you were compelled to leave suddenly, as many folk have been, and simply take what you could carry, what would you choose? If you have small children, the answer's simple. But what else? You will be walking for days, weeks, months. Only the strongest and least burdened will survive. What is most precious to you? What is it that holds your memories?

Exile in Babylon is hard to imagine. Away from home. It's not voluntary. It's not a holiday – not ten days with a package deal, with a couple of cultural visits thrown in. This was real. They were helpless, torn away by overwhelming force and taken to a strange land against their will, taking only what they could carry.

It was a long trek, 500 miles east. Many would not survive a journey like that. And when they got there? Well the Babylonians weren't totally cruel – there were no prison camps – they gave them land to settle on, and to cultivate their own gardens. They gave them work to do and as time went by, allowed them a lot of local freedom – but still it wasn't home. Nothing was the same and their memories, though painful and overwhelming, had to be suppressed enabling them to begin the planting of their new lives.

Meditation

I can see it now.
Another news story.
A distant war.
Familiar scenes,
I pause
and watch.

Homes on fire,
skies filled with smoke
and cries of the dying.
Ragged groups,
survivors,
stumbling in and out
through fractured rubble,
moving away.
Moving on,
but to what?

Exile,
a new reality
for your chosen people.
And where is their God?
Where are you, Lord?
Your promises broken?
Your protection withdrawn?
Left behind,
with their broken dreams?
Huddled together
not knowing when it would end,
belongings in dusty cartloads
they entered a strange land.
Yet your plan remained.
You were with them,
though unseen and perhaps unheard,
suffering with them,
present still.

Prayer

Lord, my life has taken
some strange turns,
though none as dramatic as this.
Yet there have been times
when I felt deserted,
Disoriented,
almost dizzy with unwelcome
change.

It's always easier in hindsight,
to look back and see your hand,
and I'm happy that I can.
To see that you were there,
standing beside,
quietly reassuring,
though I didn't always hear you,
or perhaps I wasn't listening.

Lord of my future,
be with me
when I walk on rocky ground.
Strengthen me
until I reach the level plains
of your provision.

The Journey

*Jehoiachin king of Judah, his mother, his attendants,
his nobles and his officials all surrendered to him.*
2 Kings 24:12

Imagine

*Everything was crashing down: the city walls laid waste by Nebuchadnezzar's
brutal army after a long and desperate siege. The people of Judah watched in
shock and grief as soldiers destroyed the king's palace, and the home of their
leaders, capturing their king as he fled, and bringing him back in shame. All
they could do was turn back to their God, but it was too late. They watched
in horror as the temple – the place where they believed that God lived – was
desecrated and looted, all its treasures, its gold and silver stolen. They watched
as the flames took hold, blotting out the sun and all their hopes.*

*Where was Judah's God? Was he unable to protect them now? Was he no
stronger than the gods of their enemies? Why did he not descend and strike his
enemies dead? Where was their God who had made promises to them in the
days when Moses had led them to freedom from slavery in Egypt? He was
the God who had promised to make them his 'treasured possession' in Exodus
chapter 19, verse 5, 'Now if you obey me fully and keep my covenant, then out
of all nations you will be my treasured possession. Although the whole earth is
mine, you will be for me a kingdom of priests and a holy nation.' And where
was the precious Ark of the Covenant? Remember, this was Jerusalem –
Jerushalom, the city of peace.*

*Then came the struggle to salvage a few precious items from the flames of their
own homes – family jewels, treasured heirlooms, precious bronze cooking pots.
They realised they were to follow in the footsteps of their priests and craftsmen,
their artists and metalworkers, their musicians, who had already been taken
away in an earlier siege to Babylon (2 Kings 24:16) – an early example of
ethnic cleansing. A journey that would take them far away, a journey of many
days, weeks, months to the east. There was a last minute scrabble for blankets
and clothing. Soon, as they walked, the road was littered with heavier items
discarded as they struggled to support the elderly and the young. Almost an
entire people taken into captivity, numb with grief and despair.*

Now fast-forward to 21st-century life – to countries overcome by violence, lost in the suffering of innocent people, and the loss of the normal order of life. And whether we are suffering or watching, we ask, "Why?" I have asked my share of questions, felt my faith their target, and often there is little or no answer, providing small comfort. There are some folk blessed with an unassailable experience of the close presence of God that no circumstance can change. I envy them, but it's not my experience. For others, like myself, all I can say is that, given time and a hanging-on in prayer – your own and other people's – even when it seems pointless, our questions settle and we find God within them. Not necessarily when we shout the loudest, but in God's own time. God is there in the suffering, even though our shouting drowns out his gentle voice.

Meditation

They say history repeats itself.
Sounds so familiar,
this story of war and loss,
the suffering of the innocent.

It seems we never learn.
For 'Justice is driven back,
and righteousness stands at a distance,
truth has stumbled in the streets,
honesty cannot enter'.*

And yet you are Redeemer.
You promise to save,
to deliver.
Plans to prosper and not to harm us.
Plans to give us a hope and a future.**
But we get in the way.
Do you have to skirt around us,
changing direction to bypass our mistakes?
Or do you weave them into the bigger story,
our humanity making new intricacies
in the pattern you create.

Whatever you do, Lord,
I am grateful.
I believe you are in control.
In spite of chaos,
I believe.
In spite of pain,
I believe.
In spite of evidence to the contrary,
I believe
that you are a good and loving God.

*Isaiah 59:14, ** Jeremiah 29:11

Prayer

Lord, you said
when we pass through the fire
it will not burn us,
that passing through the waters
you will be with us,
and through the rivers
we will not be overwhelmed.
Undefeated,
we will stand.
We are not to fear
this day or any other.
With a growing joy,
I can face today
and leave my tomorrows with you.
Thank you.

The Hanging Gardens of Babylon

By the rivers of Babylon we sat down
and wept when we remembered Zion.
Psalm 137:1–4

And after the long journey, the dust and heat of the long road, the pain of looking back to what had been, they finally reach their destination. Strangers in a strange land, deserted, as they thought, by their God, they must have been helped by the sight of those taken into exile earlier. They were in Babylon, today's Iraq. Historians place Babylon near the present day Al-Hillah, Babil.

Babylon was part of the Fertile Crescent, land watered by the two rivers, the Tigris and the Euphrates. Mention Babylon today and what's the first thing we think of? The Hanging Gardens. One of the Ancient Wonders of the World. There are many wonderful writings by ancient historians describing the Gardens in great detail. They did exist. Archaeologists have successfully unearthed the foundations.

We are told that Nebuchadnezzar built the gardens to alleviate the deep homesickness of his wife, Amytis, daughter of the King of the Medes, who longed for her home in Persia. She had come from a green and mountainous land to the flat and sun-baked stretches of Babylon. A political marriage, a tool for the alliance of two great powers. I wonder if it helped her, or did it make her long even more for the reality of home. For Amytis, this too was exile. Not as desperate perhaps as the people of Judah, and much more comfortable, but the pain of loss was the same. This was not her choice.

The Gardens were raised above the level of the land, to give the impression of a mountain. Great stone slabs were used – unheard of in Babylon for building – to provide the foundations and prevent erosion of the soil by water. On top of these were arched vaults at different levels, laid out like a theatre. The terraced roofs were supported by strong stone beams, covered in reeds laid in bitumen, followed by two layers of sun-baked bricks, and finally a layer of lead to stop water flowing through. Onto this complex structure was laid topsoil deep enough 'to take the largest of plants and trees'.

Rain was scarce in Babylon, so the water had to be lifted up from the Euphrates to the topmost terrace allowing it to flow down the gardens. We are told that conduits followed the steps through the garden taking the water up continuously, but the mechanism remains a mystery. The highest vault was as high as the city walls. I can see Amytis standing alone, looking out in the direction of home, wondering if she would ever return.

In 450 BC the Greek historian, Herodotus, wrote, "Babylon surpasses in splendour any city in the known world." It must have looked wonderful, this oasis of green plants tumbling over the cool slabs of stone, trees reaching high, a new Eden, a great green hill rising up, step on step over a flat and featureless landscape.

I doubt that this garden helped the Jews with their loss either. It would simply remind them of home. Painful memories of their city on a hill. Their Temple, the home of God. And of their captivity. And I wonder did they ever look back to their own creation story of the beautiful garden and ask why this had happened to them?

Did life for them settle into some sort of routine? People say you can get used to anything given enough time. Perhaps on the surface. They were given work. Structure to their day, not of their own choosing but there must have been some sort of rhythm to their new life that helped time to pass.

"Come on, get your harps out. Sing us one of your songs. Let's hear what you can do." And later the psalmist remembers it all, writes it down. "By the rivers of Babylon, we sat down and wept when we remembered..." They were homesick. And when their captors demanded happy songs, it was too much. Their tears flowed like the great rivers nearby.

Meditation

They asked us to sing.
Here, by the river.
They asked us to sing,
to fill strange hearts
with joy.

But we could not,
would not.

We tried.
We held our instruments
in trembling hands,
as they waited
with the cold, hard stares
of the conqueror,
of those who demand all
from the conquered.

We tried.
And then we remembered
all we had lost.
A thousand faces crowding in,
the dead,
the lost,
those left behind.

We remembered the beauty.
The shade of tall green trees,
soft grass beneath,
the sweetest air that spoke of home –
of flowers and spice,
of oil and wine,
of soft baked bread,
and peace to lie down.

And so –
we could not sing.
As grief swelled up,
spilling out
on broken hearts,
we could not sing.
Tears came
and washed away the foreign dust
that clung to our skin
exposing the rawness of grief
once more.

Tears came
with emotion unbidden
and we remembered you.
And for one fleeting moment
we felt a whisper,
an echo of a time that once was.
And then the shadow fell again.

But shadows fade,
and come and go,
and joy will surround once more,
and we will worship you again
on your holy mountain.

Prayer

Lord,
when all is unfamiliar
and not of my choosing,
stay near.

When I am far from home
and strangeness surrounds,
bring comfort
in a stranger's land.

When doubts flood in
and memory twists
the journey of your love for me,
remind me
of your promise
that you will never leave me
or forsake me.

I will walk in hope
and wait for better days.

Dreams of Home

*How can we sing songs of the Lord
while in a foreign land?*
Psalm 137:4

Home was just a dream. Daily life was strange, alien. A different language filled the air, and an unfamiliar culture surrounded them. They were living in a wilderness because God seemed far away. 'How can we sing the Lord's song in a foreign land?' One more thing made it even harder for them – their misunderstanding of the nature of their God. Like other nations they thought their God was a national figure who was somehow limited to his home territory. Now they were in exile, they believed God wasn't with them anymore. He was back in Jerusalem. They couldn't worship him in Babylon. They couldn't sing the 'Lord's song' in a strange land.

They were abandoned, or so it seemed. On their own, no one to help. Depression can make you feel that way. It's in the Psalmist's song. Look at Psalm 137:5,6: "If I forget you, O Jerusalem, may my right hand forget its skill. May my tongue cling to the roof of my mouth if I do not remember you, if I do not consider Jerusalem my highest joy." They lose their creativity. 'My right hand may lose its skill'. All the craftsmen, the artists, the musicians find they can no longer create. Their hearts were broken, with little urge to face life and live it.

It can happen to Christians. There can be times when we seem to live in exile, in a place where God isn't present. When the wheels come off our prayer life, we begin to wobble. Spiritually dry, we feel as if our prayers bounce back at us.

When it happened to the Jews, their homesickness, their longing and sadness turned to anger. They cursed Babylon. It's not nice, is it? But better out than in. In the same way our anger has to be acknowledged and sometimes expressed before we can get rid of it. And, only when we get rid of it, can we begin the process of forgiveness. It is forgiveness that can neutralise the poison of 'the corroding memories of past events,' as Donald Coggan, Archbishop of Canterbury, 1974–80, once put it. After the anger, the memory of past hurts has to be offered to God and left with him. Easy to say. Harder to do. 'Offered to God and left there?' God seems so far away. But he isn't. He's still close at hand. But if he's close by, why do we feel this way?

First, let's get blame out of the way. There's little point looking for someone to hold responsible. It could just be circumstances making life difficult. The Jews didn't go into exile voluntarily. They were in the hands of forces they couldn't control. It was something they just had to live through with all the patience they could find.

But can it be something in our own lives that puts God at a distance? Do we let the world and our own fears and wants get in the way? Do we hang on and repeat the disobedience that resulted in Adam and Eve losing their place in the Garden? Sad, but even if we have put God at a distance there is no point wasting time feeling guilty. Feelings of guilt use up energy which we could put to better use. Whether we recognise God's presence or not, he is still with us and he still loves us.

Meditation

It can happen so slowly,
a loss of faith.
A falling away
from old traditions
and precious belief.
Circumstances change,
though not of our making,
and anger displaces that still small voice.

Our place of worship
suddenly fills with words that confuse
and unsettle.
We long for comfort and finding none, turn away.

And yet once we have tasted
your exceptional, undeniable and undeserved love,
nothing else will do.
Once exiled, we can only turn,
and return to you.

Our hearts leap,
and like the promise of spring,
we feel your mercy.
You alone are God.
You alone can heal us.

Prayer

Lord, you and I,
we've been together a while.
At times it's been easy,
walking together,
feeling so sure of your presence.

And then a sudden shift,
and something's changed.
I'm not so sure
of anything any more.
Things I once believed
sit uneasily with me now.
People around me
seem to have it all sewn up.
Faith explained and understood.

Lord, teach me to wait
in times like these,
to hold on to my fragile faith.
'Breathe on me, breath of God'
for I know I am nothing without you.

Exiled

...our captors asked for songs...songs of joy
Psalm 137:3

There is a deep sense of longing in all of us that is part of our human condition. We were created by God, for God. There's a sense in which we have all been exiles since the time of Adam and Eve. All living away from home and longing to return to that closeness with God in the Garden.

Saint Augustine said, "Longing is the heart's treasury. The whole life of the good Christian is a holy longing. What you desire ardently, as yet you do not see... by withholding of the vision, God extends the longing; through longing he extends the soul, by extending it, he makes room in it... So...let us long because we are to be filled... That is our life, to be exercised by longing."

But within this longing, we are not abandoned. Yes it can feel that way. As I write this I am listening to a CD, an old spiritual, 'Sometimes I feel like a motherless child...' We can feel orphaned but no, wherever we go, whatever our exile, God is with us. Emmanuel. When we feel he is far away, it may be that we are facing the wrong direction. And our exile ends when we turn around and face the future. We have a God who cares, who promised to Abraham, to Isaac and to Jacob that he would lead them and always be with them. He promises the same to us. He does not abandon us.

These words were apparently found on the desk of the famous philosopher, Bertrand Russell, after his death. He was an avowed atheist. 'At the centre of me is always and eternally a terrible pain, a curious and wild pain, a searching for something transfigured and infinite, the Beatific Vision, God. I do not find it. I do not think it is to be found, but the love of it is my life.'

Whilst I find these words deeply sad, I cannot help but believe that God would have met with him. In the last moments of his life, surely one, who throughout his life, had such a deep and authentic longing for a God he did not find, would be rewarded by the God who loved him so much. He waits for us, and he will be found by us.

Meditation

Throughout our lives,
a single thread,
leading,
drawing us
through darkness
and through light.

The deepest longing,
poignantly familiar
yet unknown,
for the loving God
we do not see.

He called us 'blessed'
those who believe
without full sight of flesh and blood.
We who believe,
yet have not seen
the dead man raised again to life,
the blind man healed,
the lame restored.

And still we yearn
for more of you.

Prayer

Lord,
when I am empty,
and drained of all I know,
fill me.

Lord,
set my heart
like a compass needle towards you.
My magnetic north,
my measure of all
that is good and true,
I have all that I need in you.

Life abundant,
pressed down.
My cup is full,
overflowing with your goodness.
My words insubstantial,
your love supreme.

Lord, you have me,
heart, mind and soul.

Facing Change

Forgetting what is behind...
Philippians 3:13

Forgetting what is behind and facing the present, living with change is sometimes the hardest thing. "For here we do not have an enduring city, but we are looking for the city that is to come." (Hebrews 13:14)

How do we face the uncertainties of life? People say, "Things aren't what they used to be." Everyday there's something new, something different. Some people thrive on change, on variety. Others wish only for the comfort and security of what they know. Neither one is wrong or right. But the one thing, the one person who doesn't change is God. And he isn't a territorial figure. He is not limited by time or space. We don't only find him in church. God doesn't wear a dog collar (though he would be easier to spot if he did). He is with us now, in our worst moments and in our best. He is and always will be the one security we have in an insecure and ever-changing world.

We are all in captivity in one way or another – if not physically then captive to our feelings and needs and wants. We are never satisfied – always restless, with feelings we find hard to express, a longing for 'something better'. These feelings are widespread today. We are followed by generation after generation searching for spirituality. Some look for it in strange places. We continue to erect bigger and better shopping malls, materially so full, yet empty of anything of real and lasting worth, encouraging a different kind of worship. But the urge, the longing, is authentic.

We are created by God for God, for fellowship with him. As Augustine of Hippo (not an animal, a place on the coast of Algeria, present-day Annaba) put it, speaking to the Lord, "You have made us for yourself, and our hearts are restless until they rest in you."

And that yearning in our hearts springs from a deep and ancient memory of the Garden. Some try to get rid of this longing by getting rid of God. "God doesn't exist," they say. But this homesickness, this longing for God, to feel his presence more closely, is a thirst for the spiritual. A thirst that is expressed in the words of this lovely 14th-century hymn, by Bianco di Siena who joined the Jesuits, an order of mystics, at the age of 17.

And so the yearning strong,
with which the souls will long,
shall far out pass the power of human telling;
for none shall guess its grace,
till he become the place
wherein the Holy Spirit makes his dwelling.

This longing is such that it can only be satisfied in the relationship and freedom that Christ offers. And he knows how it feels. Jesus was an exile. He left home and came into a fallen world to help us find the way back.

And God is always searching, looking for us – as the father looked for the prodigal son. Day after day he scanned the far horizon for the sight of the son who had turned away from him.

Jesus said, "Behold I stand at the door and knock." And actually the wonderful thing is, the Holy Spirit is already within us, creating the yearning, and working with us and within us to bridge the gap that we have created, to open the door to the Garden once more. The words of another old spiritual puts it this way, "Every time I hear the Spirit moving in my heart I will pray."

But however close our relationship grows, the yearning never ceases because, as the writer Henri J.M. Nouwen* states, we are 'Always struggling to discover the fullness of love, always yearning for the complete truth. We've only been given a taste of God, of Love and Truth.' We will spend our lives continuing to follow wherever that yearning leads us and maybe that has to satisfy us for now.

*Henri J.M. Nouwen, *Dutch-born priest and writer, 1932–1996.*

Meditation

Lord, it puzzles me
that the more I experience you
the greater my longing becomes.
The sweet taste of your Spirit,
the word that leaps from the page,
the prayerful coincidence,
the whisper of your voice
all take me to a greater longing.
I am at once satisfied
and hungry to my core.

Prayer

*Lord, let this longing
grow and deepen,
always leading me on
into the mystery that is you.*

*Your eternity within,
keep me mindful
of your gift of life today,
as I follow you
once again.*

Three
The Garden of Commitment

Reading: Esther 1:1–12

This is what happened during the time of Xerxes, the Xerxes who ruled over 127 provinces stretching from India to Cush: At that time King Xerxes reigned from his royal throne in the citadel of Susa, and in the third year of his reign he gave a banquet for all his nobles and officials. The military leaders of Persia and Media, the princes, and the nobles of the provinces were present.

For a full 180 days he displayed the vast wealth of his kingdom and the splendour and glory of his majesty. When these days were over, the king gave a banquet, lasting seven days, in the enclosed garden of the king's palace, for all the people from the least to the greatest who were in the citadel of Susa. The garden had hangings of white and blue linen, fastened with cords of white linen and purple material to silver rings on marble pillars. There were couches of gold and silver on a mosaic pavement of porphyry, marble, mother-of-pearl and other costly stones. Wine was served in goblets of gold, each one different from the other, and the royal wine was abundant, in keeping with the king's liberality. By the king's command each guest was allowed to drink with no restrictions, for the king instructed all the wine stewards to serve each man what he wished.

Queen Vashti also gave a banquet for the women in the royal palace of King Xerxes.

On the seventh day, when King Xerxes was in high spirits from wine, he commanded the seven eunuchs who served him – Mehuman, Biztha, Harbona, Bigtha, Abagtha, Zethar and Carcas – to bring before him Queen Vashti, wearing her royal crown, in order to display her beauty to the people and nobles, for she was lovely to look at. But when the attendants delivered the king's command, Queen Vashti refused to come. Then the king became furious and burned with anger.

The King gave a banquet

Imagine

What an empire! One hundred and twenty seven provinces. Stretching from India in the east to Cush [Egypt and Ethiopia] in the west.

The whole story of Esther here fires the imagination. Can you picture it? A great garden. Walled in for shelter from the heat of the wind. A very private place. It was prepared for an extravagant banquet. A marquee like no other marquee. Read verses 6 to 8. Money was no object. It sounds like a Hollywood blockbuster. The king had displayed his wealth for all to see over 180 days, and then gave a feast that lasted seven days. It describes everything except the plants. There were flowering trees and shrubs, the sounds of running water from streams and fountains. (The Persians made great use of water.) Gold in abundance, floors of marble and precious stones, couches of gold and silver. Unimaginable wealth.

We have moved on 60 years or so from the mass deportation of the Jews to Babylon. Things have changed. Now Nebuchadnezzar is no more and Babylon has been conquered by another great army – the Persians led by Emperor Cyrus. Cyrus was tough but more benign. He gave the Jews their freedom and many went back to Jerusalem to rebuild their city and Temple – but that's another story. Some stayed on in Babylon – they had been there now for several generations. They were settled, and Jerusalem would be a strange place to them. As strange a place as Babylon was to their grandparents who'd been brought here by force. How circumstances can change if you give them time.

Back to the garden, but not the one in Babylon. Xerxes had built a new city, Susa, and that is where this feast took place. Cyrus's successor, King Xerxes, was having a party. And what a party. On the seventh day it says, 'King Xerxes was in high spirits from wine.' That was a polite way of putting it. I suppose you never say a king is drunk. But he was. Not surprisingly. And so were his guests. 'Each guest was allowed to drink in his own way.' That might have been his first mistake. It's not a pretty picture, the king, all the officials, all drunk. Can you imagine the hangover when it's all over?

A rather different picture from the wedding at Cana. I can't see Jesus adding to the drunkenness, can you? And when men are drunk, they think they are full of wisdom. They know just what to do to put the world right. Drunken men talking about their women. "I've got the most beautiful woman in the entire world," says the king – if you could understand his slurred consonants. No one disagrees but the king says, "I'll show you..." and he calls for his officials to bring Queen Vashti to show her off to his guests. He's not really praising her. The very opposite. He's not treating her with respect as a human being, only wanting to display her as another of his possessions – like a prize cow. Not a great picture but a common one. A powerful man treading all over the feelings of people in his power.

But the queen is a tough lady. Courageous. She has her pride and refuses to come, refuses to be paraded in front of so many men. Good for her. She was standing up for her rights, what few rights women had, but it got her into deep trouble.

The king was furious, losing face in public, his pride was hurt. What should he do? And whatever he does no one is going to disagree with the king in that state. And even when he was sober again and the anger has subsided, and the hangover dispelled, the king calls his advisers – the cabinet – and they see an opportunity, they gang up on the queen.

"We can't let her get away with that... every woman will do it." They egg on King Xerxes and Queen Vashti is deposed, exiled from the King's presence. I wonder, did she love him? Women in those days were often simply used as a way of forging alliances between powerful countries. Was she upset by the end of this relationship, or more upset that she was forced to leave precious friends and familiarity? A life-changing decision for her and consequences she would have to live with for the rest of her life.

Meditation

It started out so well.
A royal occasion.
A thousand foreign guests
called to the beauty of a garden
to celebrate the wealth of a King.

It started out so well.
Lavish hospitality,
of food and of wine.
The power and the pleasure
in one moment
so unbalanced.

Seven days it took
to spoil a king.
Seven days to banish a queen
for the saving of his foolish pride.
Seven days to regret
and see with fresh eyes
the enormity of what he had done.

But you had a bigger plan –
the saving of a people.
Your people, chosen long ago,
and so the story unfolds.

Prayer

Lord, save me from my mistakes,
when I am full of pride,
and my judgement's unreliable.

I mean well.
We always do, don't we?
Justifying actions which,
in the clear light of day,
look muddied and full of regret.

Let me learn to pause,
to see with your eyes.
My intentions laid bare
in honest submission.

Let me do no harm, Lord,
only good,
for your name's sake.

The King needs a Queen

Later when the anger of King Xerxes had
subsided, he remembered Vashti and what she
had done, and what he had decreed about her.
Esther 2:1

The king 'remembered' Vashti. Does this mean he regretted his actions?
Did he remember her, or only her actions, her refusal to come? I'd like to
think he felt some degree of regret or at least, embarrassment over his very
public decision. Decisions made in anger are often clouded and poorly judged.
But the king needs a queen so what is he to do? Organise a beauty contest,
for that is what this amounts to. Miss World 480 BC. The most beautiful
unmarried women in every province were to be brought into the court at Susa.

Enter Mordecai and Esther. They were from a Jewish family who had stayed
on in Babylon. Mordecai's great-grandfather had been taken into exile from
Jerusalem by the Babylonian army. Read Esther chapter 2 verses 5–7. Esther
was the orphaned daughter of a cousin, looked after by Mordecai. 'Esther'
means 'star' and that is what she would become. Mordecai enters Esther
into the great contest without revealing she is Jewish. (Wouldn't they know?
No checks on her background?) Mordecai forbade her from revealing her
background. He knew the trouble it could cause.

To cut a long story short – it was a long process before she was presented
to the king, 12 months of beauty treatments – she wins. "Let the girl who
pleases the king be queen instead of Vashti." So easily replaced. Queen Vashti
is no more and Esther becomes Queen. A true rags to riches story. She was
obviously very special. We are told: 'Esther won the favour of everyone who
saw her.'

'And they lived happily ever after.' Well, no, not quite. There is a plot to
assassinate the king. Mordecai hears of it and alerts Esther who is able to
tell the king. The plotters are dealt with and Mordecai is given the credit. But
then petty jealousies and pride get in the way. The King is misled and orders
the massacre of all the Jews in his kingdom. Mordecai somehow slips past
security and comes to Queen Esther. "Do something. Go to the King. Speak
for your people. You're the only one who can." She is frightened, terrified, and
rightly so. There are rules and customs. Anyone approaching the king without
his permission will be put to death. Esther remembers Queen Vashti. She tries
to ignore the situation, tries to walk by on the other side. Are we sometimes

guilty of that? 'Why should I get involved? It's nothing to do with me.' But it was, and she gathers her courage. Was it Mordecai's challenge to her?

'And who knows but that you have come to royal position for such a time as this?' (*Esther 4:14*). For such a time as this. Whatever it was, she says yes. But not before asking him to get all the Jews to fast and pray for three days and three nights. She knew the seriousness of what she was about to do. She also knew the power of prayer over the reputation of an angry King. "When this is done, I will go to the King... and if I perish, I perish." That's courage.

Meditation

For such a time as this.
The challenge laid out.
The stakes are high.
The risk of one life
for the rescue of many.

For such a time as this,
when justice turns away,
and wicked men are plotting
a genocide
with royal approval.

For such a time as this
you ask for her obedience.
And seeing the greater need
and knowing a Greater Power,
she enters
and asks for mercy.

Prayer

Lord,
Can I find the courage,
when you challenge me to action,
to speak out where others won't,
to find my voice
in the face of
the world's misuse of authority?

Or shall I look away
and hope for someone else,
someone better suited
like Moses hoped for Aaron?
But yet he went,
and so did Esther.

Give me courage, Lord,
when it really matters.
Give me eyes to see the
bigger picture,
to see beyond myself.
Give me a heart that will not fail you.
A heart that believes
it is 'for such a time as this'.
I'll take the next step
and trust you for the future.

The King's Delight

When he saw Queen Esther standing in
the court he was pleased with her...
Esther 5:2

Esther succeeds. Read the whole story. It's a fantastic tale of intrigue and revenge that we don't have time or space for here. The Jews are saved. And with them God's purposes for his people are saved. That's the way the writer sees it. They're preserved for greater things.

But that was more than 25 centuries ago. It's hard to relate to today. A romantic story in some parts but where is its relevance now? Bruce Feiler in his book *Walking the Bible* talks of 'the Bible's effortless ability to reinvent itself for every generation and every new way of searching.' I like that. It's the truth. We can always find some relevance to where we are in life, always learn, always observe something valuable. That's the beauty of it. God-breathed. God-inspired. Whether you believe that literally or not, God's Spirit moves through each page. If we are listening.

But first a question. Are there such things as coincidences? As we read the whole story, several times things just seem to happen. Queen Vashti just happens to anger the king and is removed. Esther just happens to win the contest and gets to be the new queen. Her uncle just happens to hear about a plot to kill the king and warns him. Later the King just happens to read something about her uncle's actions, and so on. So often in life things happen without any apparent reason, but looking back on them we see a pattern. Just an accident, or can we see God at work? Søren Kierkegaard, the 19th-century Danish philosopher and theologian, said, "You can only understand life backwards but you have to live it forwards."

Strangely, this is the only book in the Bible in which God is never specifically mentioned. There is no reference to him or to worship but there are hints. Fasting is mentioned, and in chapter 4 verse 14: 'for such a time as this...' implies Esther's position at court is no accident. Arranged by a higher power.

The implication right through the story is that God is at work and is actively transforming the situation. His presence is to be reckoned with, even when he is not acknowledged. This is the world he created, the wonderful garden he planted – it's got a bit weedy but it's still his – and he's still in it with us. Still at work, but often through the efforts of individual people, in ways we can't always recognise.

And that's another thing. God tends to work through people, through our own efforts, and he uses the most unlikely people to transform things such as Esther, an immigrant Jewish orphan, a woman.

Fast-forward to Jesus' choice of disciples. You might say, "Oh they were special." Were they? Peter – the rough fisherman, often getting things wrong. How much education did he have? And Thomas, famous forever for his very public doubt as to whether Jesus was alive or not. And what about Mary Magdalene with her rather dubious past?

These were ordinary people made extraordinary by their closeness to Jesus, by their choices, their willingness to be used and become part of God's purposes. We have to take the initiative. Do we sometimes waste time sitting back and waiting for 'it' to happen? We have to choose. We are all free – we can say yes, we can say no. There may be a point when our courage and our faith fails. "Not me Lord, I can't do it..." Moses at the burning bush. Esther caught up in great things far beyond her power. Yet, as Paul writes: 'God chose the foolish things of the world to shame the wise: God chose the weak things of the world to shame the strong.' (*I Corinthians 1:27*)

I suggest we don't lack the potential. We lack the will. The weak only become strong by opening themselves up to the transforming power of God.

There is a danger of false humility. 'I'm no use to God. I'm not good enough.' True. None of us is. What matters isn't what we are, but who God is. It can be an excuse for doing nothing. (What might have happened if the Samaritan had also passed by on the other side?) We need to say 'Yes' to God a little more often. Look at what those disciples were like immediately after the crucifixion. A frightened group of men and women. Hardly a promising group on which to found a church – The Church. But what a change after the resurrection. They were able to face the power of Rome and not falter.

71

Meditation

You made some strange choices, Lord.
Ordinary people without a track record.
People from the poorest of backgrounds,
hardly fitting the job description.

Into the middle of explosive authority
you send a woman,
with small experience of life
to fight for the survival of a nation.

Into a palace,
where men cheat and lie
in their lust for power,
you send a woman
to speak for truth.

Into the face of a law
that could silence with death,
you sent a woman,
and she stood in her royal robes
and waited.

And the king saw her courage
and it pleased him.
He held out the golden sceptre
to her and her people.

And once again your people are saved,
and once again history is changed.

Prayer

Lord,
it's easy to think
that the little I do
is of no consequence to you,
that the world will not change because of me.

Forgive me for lack of action,
when I fear I'll waste my time
and no one will see the little I do.

But I do believe I have a choice,
and I have a part to play.
Whether small or big,
it's the part you have given to me.
So Lord,
whatever I can do, I will do.
with your help.

For Such a Time...

And who knows but that you have come
to royal position for such a time as this?
Esther 4:14

For God to use us we have to be involved in the world. Esther was effective because she agreed to get involved. She wanted to walk away at first. It was a terrifying situation. But she still agreed. There is the temptation for us as Christians to back away from the world, to pull up the drawbridge and hide behind verses such as: 'Do not conform any longer to the pattern of this world' (*Romans 12:2*), as an excuse not to get involved.

I remember being in East Berlin when it was under the Communists and talking with Ralph Daaman, a Baptist leader who said, "In the beginning I used to wish I was somewhere else but I slowly began to realise that we were where God wanted us to be and where he could use us."

It is so easy to wish we were somewhere else in difficult times, in fact it's probably our first thought. But maybe we are just where we are needed. It's easy to say and more challenging to live out. Jesus said we are the leaven, the yeast that gets into the dough and transforms it. Yeast can only work when it is mixed in. I know from experience, we have a bread machine. You know that you've forgotten to put the yeast in when you are confronted with a small and disappointingly heavy lump of cooked dough. We can only influence the world when we live in it. So there we are – but not quite.

How do you really see the book of Esther? When I began to prepare this study I saw it as a wonderful story of a beautiful young woman (no man can resist that), taken from obscurity to riches who, through her courage, saved her people from death. God choosing the weak. But I wasn't at ease with what I'd written. It niggled me. Driving to the Garden Centre one day (very appropriate), it suddenly dawned on me that there is a deeper level to the whole story. That underlying it all is a disturbing picture of the misuse of power – at all levels. And I believe that's what this story means to tell us.

First, the king. The feasting is a demonstration of his power: 'Wealth, splendour and glory.' He's a despot. He has absolute control. Life and death in his hands. Then he misuses his authority by abusing his queen. Putting her on display. Trampling on her feelings and her personality. And, when she refuses to be trodden on, he reacts angrily and punishes her with banishment.

Esther is very different. She has no power or influence at first. An orphan entered into a contest by her uncle to be part of the king's harem. (Sounds like a great beginning for a movie.) But when her people are in danger of a massacre – a blatant abuse of human power – she intervenes and uses her new influence with courage for good. She saves her people. A happy ending. Or is it?

Then comes the saddest part of all. A sort of 'P.S.' for all of us. The Jews are rescued from danger, but take terrible revenge. They massacre their enemies. You can read it in chapter 9. The persecuted take the power the king gives them and become the persecutors. This people who had known war and suffering, who were descendants of a people taken into exile and who know the evil results of the misuse of power, now use it themselves. They are possessed by the evil that threatened them.

Even Esther gets involved in the punishment. Look at Chapter 9 again. The influence she had with the king that she used for good, she now uses badly in punishing the family of her enemy at court. A frightening reminder perhaps, that power can corrupt even the most well-meaning. Think about the way we use the power we have. The 'jobsworth' parking attendant, the unco-operative receptionist, our roles within family at home and church.

Living with power is like walking on a slippery slope. And the only protection we have from sliding into its misuse is our closeness to God. When God takes the weak and the foolish of the world and gives them strength, it is only to be used for good. Remember Jesus' last words before his ascension, "You will receive power when the Holy Spirit comes upon you; and you will be my witnesses..." Witnesses to the power of love and forgiveness and sacrifice.

Meditation

A happy ending?
Maybe for some,
but power corrupts
and the saved people
became the slayers.

How sad,
that your beautiful purpose
was stained by uncontrollable
revenge.

How sad,
that there was no reconciliation,
only a lust for blood.

God, forgive.
It's easy for us to judge them
from a position of comfort.
I don't understand,
but I know
without a doubt
that you are a just God
and your purposes remain
good and true,
in spite of us.

Prayer

Lord,
Be with those who have the power
to change worlds.
Be with those who meet with kings
and leaders,
who take your presence into
legislation and fight for justice.
Be with those who work unseen
with the poor and the voiceless.

Lord,
Be with those who lead your people,
with dreams of unity
and reconciliation.
Be with us,
who doubt the value of our position,
and the little influence we have.
'Faith the size of a mustard seed',
that's all you ask.
Let us believe today
and use whatever power we have
for good.

Four

The Garden of Sacrifice

Reading: Matthew 26:36–46

Then Jesus went with his disciples to a place called Gethsemane, and he said to them, "Sit here while I go over there and pray." He took Peter and the two sons of Zebedee along with him, and he began to be sorrowful and troubled. Then he said to them, "My soul is overwhelmed with sorrow to the point of death. Stay here and keep watch with me."

Going a little farther, he fell with his face to the ground and prayed, "My Father, if it is possible, may this cup be taken from me. Yet not as I will, but as you will."

Then he returned to his disciples and found them sleeping. "Could you men not keep watch with me for one hour?" he asked Peter. "Watch and pray so that you will not fall into temptation. The spirit is willing, but the body is weak."

He went away a second time and prayed, "My Father, if it is not possible for this to be taken away unless I drink it, may your will be done."

When he came back, he again found them sleeping, because their eyes were heavy. So he left them and went away once more and prayed the third time, saying the same thing.

Then he returned to the disciples and said to them, "Are you still sleeping and resting? Look, the hour is near, and the Son of Man is betrayed into the hands of sinners. Rise, let us go! Here comes my betrayer!"

Watch and Pray

*Then Jesus went with his disciples to a place called
Gethsemane, and he said to them, "Sit here
while I go over there and pray..."*
Matthew 26:36

Gethsemane. There were few gardens in Jerusalem; there was not much space in a city crowded on a hill. King Herod had a pleasure garden down in the Kidron valley near the Pool of Shiloam, and I imagine a garden of sorts for Pontius Pilate, the Roman Governor. And a few gardens perhaps on the Mount of Olives where the rich relaxed.

But there was one garden on the hillside that Jesus knew. A garden where Jesus and the disciples often met. A lovely thought. Jesus and the disciples enjoying quiet moments under ancient olive trees. Maybe picnicking in the sun, away from the turmoil and noise of the crowded city and the demands of the people. The downside was that Judas knew where to find him.

Luke says in chapter 22 verse 39 that after supper they 'went out as usual' to Gethsemane, a garden of olive trees on the western slope of the Mount of Olives. We don't know who owned it. Maybe a secret disciple. There must have been many other unnamed helpers – the owner of the garden, the one who lent Jesus the donkey, the owner of the Upper Room, and surely many others. People whose names we'll never know, but men and women who had the privilege of doing something for Jesus. Maybe people who gave Jesus the inspiration for the story of the Good Samaritan. People who didn't walk by on the other side of the road but stopped and listened and helped. Thank God for the unnamed helpers who have influenced our lives. There are many for all of us – people willing to contribute in quiet ways, to listen when others were too busy, to help with the routine and unglamorous jobs within church life.

I often wish I had lived then and seen it all first-hand. I have great sympathy with Thomas. He needed to see and touch the risen Christ, and Jesus met him at the point of his need. As he does with us. We might all wish we had been there with him but we cannot choose the time or place of our birth. We are believers in spite of not having seen him. We believe in hope of things to come. We see a mix of the Kingdom of God here and now, and the 'not yet'. Did they all believe when they saw the miraculous? I doubt it. Some will always choose to disbelieve the evidence in front of them. And there were miracles, day after day. It is our choice. Whether to be with him and believe.

Meditation

I wish I'd been there,
one of your followers,
right from the start.
Called by a friend to come
and hear the Teacher.

I wish I'd been there
to see you heal the sick,
open sightless eyes,
and straighten twisted limbs.
To see them leap and dance
in holy disbelief
and utter joy.

I wish I'd been there,
following you through heat of day
to the garden on a hill
where we would doze
and dream of miracles
and hope for understanding.

I wish I'd been there
to watch the loaves and fish,
a gift from a hope-filled boy,
fill the mouths of thousands
on a hot and dusty day.

People talked of the Messiah –
as your light shone
on dusty and forgotten dreams.
And the crowds grew larger
as the Pharisees watched in anger.

I'm glad I wasn't there
when darkness came
and overtook all hopes
of a free Jerusalem
and a victorious world.
I couldn't have borne to see
your pain
as you stumbled with your cross.
I couldn't have watched with your
mother Mary
and your beloved John
as your life ebbed away
and the sun hid its face.

But oh to have been there
when you returned.

Prayer

Lord, we cannot change the timing of our birth.
We cannot predict what will be
and how life will end,
but whatever comes
let it be with you.

Set me on fire again
with that first love
for you, my Messiah.
Lift my hopes out of the dust
and bring me to life in all its fullness.

A Place of Suffering

He took Peter and the two sons of Zebedee...
Matthew 26:37

Imagine

*That night after supper, Jesus took all the disciples – except Judas – to
Gethsemane. They pick their way through the streets in the early dusk, out of
the city gate and across the valley. The full moon shows the rough path ahead,
up the Mount of Olives to the Garden. It was more a walled orchard than what
we think of as a garden today. Gethsemane means 'olive press'. A garden full
of olive trees, bent, twisted and gnarled with age. A place of moonlight and
shadows as the breeze moves the leaves on the trees. Deep shadows as though
nature is trying to cover up and hide the suffering that lay ahead.*

*They went together, and as they entered the garden, Jesus told most of them to
sit down and wait. Only Peter and James and John went on with him. Jesus is
troubled. He tells them, too, to sit down – I see them sitting with their backs to
a tree, wrapping their cloaks around them against the cool breeze. They whisper
for a few moments, trying to understand what Jesus had said, then shrug,
mutter a prayer and settle down to wait. It's late. In the darkness, just a few
dim lights across the valley in the city. No one else is about.*

*Jesus goes on a little way, 'a stone's throw' – so it was a fairly large garden
– and drops to the ground. There are a few moments in the Gospel where I
wonder if I have the right to watch and listen. This seems to be one of them.
Such a private moment for Jesus and I feel I'm an intruder, an eavesdropper.
Jesus was more than troubled. Overwhelmed with the thought of what lay
ahead. Jesus knows what is coming. How detailed his knowledge was we'll never
know, but he foresaw the agony ahead. Verse 38: "My soul is overwhelmed with
sorrow to the point of death."*

*The pain gives birth to questions. "Father," Jesus asks, "Isn't there another way?
You're God, can't we find an alternative? Does it have to be like this?" It is in
times of pain when most of us ask this question – although I doubt if we're ever
faced with this degree of suffering. And when our pain and questioning come,
the fact that Jesus knows what it feels like can help. No easy comfort. It still
hurts. But he does know and in our times of pain, it is deeply precious and
something to hold on to, sometimes the only thing to hold on to.*

Meditation

You were with friends,
in that dark
and troubled place.
Air thick with fear
and a knowing dread
of what was to come.

You were with friends
tried and trusted,
but as you agonized,
pleaded
and wept with the Father,
in the darkness beyond,
they slept.

Did they not notice your pain?
Could they not see
the depths of conflict
inside your very soul?
They slept.
With their cloaks wrapped around,
their only concern
the cold wind
and intermittent rain.

You were alone.
And yet
you stood,
facing what was to come,
your love brushing aside
their lack.
You knew this journey
was for you
and you alone.

Only your feet
could tread
the twisted path ahead.
Only your hands
held out in submission
to the brutality of your captors.
Only your head
crowned by barbarous thorns.

You embraced the Father's will
and changed our world
forever.

Prayer

Lord,
what can I say?
My words so lacking,
my heart so full.
You gave your life for me
and I,
flawed,
empty
and profoundly grateful
kneel at your feet.

Your Will, Not Mine

"If it is possible, let this cup pass away from me."
Matthew 26:39

I'm sure Jesus didn't want to die. Only 33 years old, in the prime of his life. He could have backed out, said 'No'. We don't really take this on board. We've heard the story so many times, and with hindsight there seems to be an inevitability about it. But Jesus could have said no. He could have turned away from the agony that was to come. God gives us all the freedom to accept or reject him, and Jesus had the same freedom we have. If his sacrifice wasn't voluntary then it would have been meaningless. Jesus had to agree to it. It was unimaginably hard.

But in these moments – the questioning and the hesitation, he says, "If it is possible, take this cup away. This cup of pain. Yet not what I will, but as you will." An acceptance that goes beyond our understanding. There are times when we all have to accept situations we don't understand. It doesn't come easily. Doubts surface and we have to face them.

Doubt and faith go together, hand in hand. One does not cancel out the other. Admitting to our doubts does not mean our faith is weaker. On the contrary, it takes courage to admit to what we don't know, to things we can't understand, and yet still believe; things we never will understand, but in spite of them our faith survives, and grows. A mysterious mix of head and heart, intellect and emotion.

This is what Paul means when he says: 'Now we see but a poor reflection as in a mirror; then we shall see face to face. Now I know in part; then I shall know fully, even as I am fully known.' (*1 Corinthians 13:12*)

In Ephesians chapter 3 verse 10, the wisdom of God is described as 'complicated and many-sided... with all its infinite variety and innumerable aspects' (*Amplified Bible*). Our problems come when we start to believe that we have the whole truth, and healthy questions are strangled by inflexibility. Faith becomes more like a brick wall, rather than like a dynamic and maturing part of our lives. Sometimes God asks more of us than we want to give, beyond our capabilities, beyond our imagining, beyond our understanding. Sometimes he asks us to endure, to persevere and still believe, to look trouble and pain in the face and step forwards with him. That's when we show courage and faith, in spite of outward circumstance and with God's help, and often in spite of how we feel.

Meditation

You asked so much of him,
more than I would give.
A shortened life.
A cruel court,
where justice was held prisoner
by prejudice and fear.

You asked so much of him,
an agony foreseen,
entered into freely.
Forsaking all else
for the love of the Father
and a broken world.
He faced fear
for the sake of a distant joy.
And that joy is his gift to us.
Not what we deserve
but grace, full and free.

Prayer

Lord, I am not brave,
preferring to sit safely
with things I know and understand.
You want my all and I hold back,
scared of losing control
of my small and comfortable life.

Lord, give me the grace
to face my doubts,
to stand established in your love,
to endure my present pain,
to look to you,
my unshakeable God.
Intent on you and you alone.
Thank you.

Unanswered Prayer

"...if it is possible... Yet not as I will, but as you will."
Matthew 26:39

We talk about answered prayer. Prayer is often answered – not always in the way we have asked – but what about unanswered prayer? Some say 'No' is an answer in itself, but I find this a little glib. Maybe it is true, but at times however hard we pray there is just silence. C.S. Lewis, writing about the days after his wife died, said it was as though his 'prayers were bouncing back from a brick wall.'

Gethsemane is the greatest example of unanswered prayer ever. We're not told of any voice from heaven reassuring Jesus. Present at baptism, but absent now. Jesus just had to accept the silence. But if God had answered in the way Jesus had asked, the whole purpose of his coming would have been lost. It is only through his death and resurrection that we find the new life he offers.

We see the same sort of acceptance in his mother, Mary, at the annunciation. When she is told that she'll be mother to Jesus, she replies to God's messenger, "Let it be to me according to your word" (*New King James Version*). I believe it was not a fatalistic shrug of the shoulders. 'Let it be – there's nothing I can do about it,' but a positive willingness to do as God wills. She too could have said 'No', and part of me wonders what would have happened if she had. Would the Angel Gabriel have gone on to another house, would he have found someone else willing, where she was not? Mary knew what was ahead. The difficult explanation, the disbelief, the horror of family reactions, and what about Joseph? Pregnancy outside marriage today no longer shocks, but in those days it was a stoning offence. She knew the consequences and yet she said 'Yes'.

Thank God, she said 'Yes'. And so may we.

Meditation

I can imagine her surprise.
An angel
in the house.
An ordinary day,
a list of jobs ahead,
a dusty road outside
in a quiet village.

And there he was,
immense,
iridescent,
straight from heaven,
and speaking to her.
And so matter-of-fact.

She was blessed.
God had noticed her.
He was going to use her
in his immortal plan,
fulfilling the prophets,
saving her people.
I can imagine the shock,
the confusion,
the 'is this really happening?'
And yet
she knew it was God.
No question.
The angel was real.
The facts were plain.
And in that moment of choice,
the world's future,
yours and mine,
hung in the balance.
As she paused for breath,
creation,
and all of heaven,
waited.

Did the earth stop turning,
just for a moment,
a millisecond's pause
in its ancient orbit?
Did the angel hold his breath?
Did time itself stand still?

And when she said "Yes,"
"be it unto me according to your will."
I can feel the universal sigh,
and hear a distant cheer,
as she took her first step
into your salvation plan.

And I am grateful.
She is truly blessed,
and through her,
so are we.
Thank you, Lord.

A. D. ASKEW

Prayer

*Lord, there are times
when my 'Yes' is easy,
costing nothing.
My heart is full
and I can see your plan.
My steps are on a level plain
and I feel you close.*

*But when darkness comes,
and I stumble on unseen rocks,
my breath uncertain
and faith and friendship
a distant thing,
will my 'Yes' stand firm?*

*Only with your help, Lord.
Even if there is no angel for me,
no vision in my kitchen,
let me know your deep
and abiding presence.*

*Thank you for all the twists and turns
in my life,
for you were there
through all.*

A Willing Spirit

"...may your will be done."
Matthew 26:42

The kingdom of God is built on 'Yes's. On positive living, not on negatives. "Your will, not mine." The Amplified version puts it this way. "Yet not my will but always yours be done." So easy to say, less easy to do, to live my life that way in the pain and difficulty of each day. Yet that is what God asks.

'Not my will, but yours.' We can have no real idea of what it cost Jesus to say that and mean it. We know it exhausted him. Luke writes of sweat '...like clots of blood dropping to the ground.' Jesus was in 'agony of mind.'

Remembering that Gethsemane means 'olive-press', Brother Ramon, a 20th-century Franciscan monk, wrote: '...it's as if Jesus were being crushed under the world's sin so that the oil of forgiveness could be poured out into the world's wounds.' A desperate picture and a desperate pain, but somehow, in and with the pain, there is hope.

Then, in the moonlight, Jesus gets up and walks back slowly to his three close friends. He finds them asleep. That must have hurt, though Luke does tell us: '...when he rose from prayer...he found them asleep, exhausted from sorrow' (*Luke 22:45*). They knew he was leaving them, and couldn't stay awake for fear of the future. (Or they chose sleep rather than face the future?) To Peter, Jesus says, "Are you asleep? Could you not keep watch for one hour?" (*Mark 14:37*). Earlier that same evening, Peter had boasted: "Even if everyone else deserts you, I will never desert you" (*Matthew 26:33, NLT*). A grand gesture. Brave words, and I'm sure he meant them. Having the strength to carry them through was a different matter. He could not have imagined that he would be tested so soon. Now he was asleep.

This is a moment when everything has been turned upside down. In the past it was the disciples needing Jesus's strength. Now Jesus is the needy one. He needs their strength but they are asleep. We can sympathise with them. Exhausted by the tension, they are bewildered by Jesus's behaviour. The pressure of the last few days, and their inability to understand much of what Jesus had been telling them, had opened them to fear. It was growing inside them, as dark as the night-sky deepening around them.

"Watch and pray, so that you will not fall into temptation." Can you fall into temptation when you are asleep? Not when we're literally asleep, but we can get careless, and be caught off-guard. 'The spirit is willing but the body is weak.' Too true for all of us. Even St Paul. Although, if I'm honest, I'm not sure the spirit is always willing. We'd like it to be. We often say it is, but our motives are always mixed. And a willing spirit is something that we struggle for. Even the psalmist found it difficult. He had to ask God: "...grant me a willing spirit" (*Psalm 51:12*). This was something Jesus struggled towards in his agony in the garden. Somehow, he found the strength to say 'Yes'. He knew what was ahead of him, and yet he chose to face it.

God help us to do the same.

Meditation

In the tension of the night,
did you hear the wind move leaf and branch
and feel damp moss as you knelt in prayer?
Did you sense your disciples slip away
into troubled sleep
the air thick with unseen powers,
and palpable fear?

Did you ever doubt the love of your father
as the terrifying future
marched up the hill?

And through it all,
did you ever wish
that your love for us,
so immense and all-encompassing
could be set aside
and bring you to a different path?

And even though
this may be true,
in spite of doubt and fear,
you chose love.
And because of your outrageous love,
I am forever thankful.

Prayer

Not my will, but yours.
I can say it easily enough
but my heart shrinks back
in case you ask for more than I can give.
Or more than I want to give.
You know I love you, Lord,
but I can be fearful,
finding it easier to hide away,
to sleep,
and ignore the challenge ahead.

You know my heart, Lord.
I want to be all
and do all I can for you.
but I fear letting you down,
falling asleep on the job,
not quite good enough.

But then I'm forgetting grace,
your Grace.
The full, free
and undeserved favour
and love of God my Father.
Your Grace covers me,
fills in the gaps,
puts a different light
on my restless understanding.
and comforts my prodigal heart.

You love me, Lord,
and simply want my 'yes'.
Today.
Now.
That is all.
And you have it.
"Yes," to all that you have for me,
with my grateful thanks.

He calls us 'Friend'

*So he left them and went away once
more and prayed the third time...*
Matthew 26:44

Twice more, he went back and prayed, which suggests that his acceptance of God's will involved a long struggle. Twice more he came back and found his friends asleep. I wonder what we sleep through in our insensitivity to others' needs? How easily we turn away from suffering and other people's pain.

When the disciples open their eyes it is to a rude awakening. To violence and betrayal. An armed and threatening crowd, unfamiliar noise and confusion. The flames from burning torches illuminate aggressive faces. And leading the crowd was Judas, one of their own. I can't hate or even begin to judge him, but think of him as a desperately sad figure who comes with head bent and eyes down, betraying Jesus with a kiss. Why a kiss? Why not simply a pointed finger? A kiss seems to double the hurt and make the betrayal worse. The pretence of love.

And Jesus calls him 'Friend'. A poignant moment. Maybe that's where we should leave our thoughts. Whatever we do, however weak our flesh, however strong or weak our willingness to follow him, however much we sleep, however far we fall, Jesus calls us 'Friend'. Peter denied him, the others ran away, but Jesus returned to them. Judas betrayed him, but Jesus called him 'Friend'. This is limitless, uncompromising love. A love which can look beyond the betrayal and look on the betrayer with unreserved compassion. A love which chooses to remain faithful, where faith has been broken. A love which can stand in the face of hatred and injustice and stay true to God's purpose. This is the love we can experience today, every day. He remains our Saviour and calls us his friends.

Meditation

What love led you to this place, Lord,
that you could stand
in the face of such evil,
to give all of yourself,
to gain all for us?

And where would I have been?
Hidden in the shadows,
or clinging to your side?
Would I have fought for you,
risking my own life,
or run in blinding panic,
not able to watch,
and powerless to change?

You knew it would happen,
and yet you chose to accept
and forgive.

And you do it still,
for every time we deny you,
or look away,
you call us 'friend'.
Your love remains
as strong and true as at the
beginning of time.

Alpha and Omega,
you do not change.

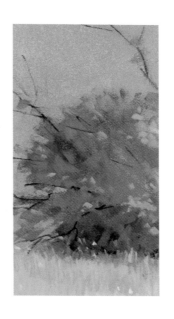

Prayer

Lord,
let my love for you,
my loving friend,
remain through all my days.
As my hair grows grey,
and my body slows,
as memory gently fades,
let me remain,
by your side.
Always.

And after the garden... Golgotha

They came to a place called Golgotha...
Matthew 27:33

I've given up trying to understand Gethsemane and the death of Jesus. First the betrayal by Judas, the moment of futile violence as a desperate disciple hits out, the soldier healed by Jesus's touch (I am amazed that even in that moment of utter darkness surrounded by blatant evil, Jesus saw a servant's wound and reached out with love to heal.) Then the mockery of his trial culminating in the horror of the crucifixion. All the theories and theologies that try to explain how our forgiveness is accomplished through the cross still leave me wondering, 'Why?' (It's a bit like biologists trying to explain why two people fall in love by analysing the biochemistry of their hormones.) I just try to accept the cross and hold onto it and the hope it gives me. The fact is enough for me. As David Jenkins, Bishop of Durham, 1984–1994, says, "Jesus is. Jesus is as he was. Therefore there is hope."

Jesus somehow opens the garden gate and leads us back into that loving relationship with God that began in Eden. I can see a strange sort of parallel. The garden of Gethsemane echoes the Eden story, the difference being that in contrast with Adam and Eve's disobedience, Jesus is 'the obedient one', 'even unto death'. The miracle is that *relationship* with God is now restored. To have Jesus as *friend* with everything that means, is enough for me to base my life on. And yours.

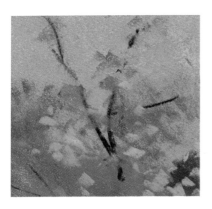

In Gethsemane

The wound healed.
The sword washed clean.
No visible sign remains.

Only the violence within
and the unknown thoughts
of the high priest's servant.
When is healing complete?

Eddie Askew, Easter 2000.

Prayer

Lord,
was his life
ever the same?
That night
of violent darkness,
when flickering lights
showed angry faces.
The searing pain
and his disbelief
as the sword did its work.
And then you touched him.
A sudden joy rushes through,
an inexplicable love,
and you were gone.

I see him then,
touching his ear,
a mix of wonder and disbelief,
his own blood still on his hand.
I see him now,
fingering the long white scar,
remembering,
with gratitude,
the loving touch
that changed his life.

Lord,
touch me now,
heal my wounds.
I don't ask for understanding,
only for your touch
to transform my life.

Five
The Garden of New Life

Reading: John 19:41 and John 20:1–18

At the place where Jesus was crucified, there was a garden, and in the
garden, a new tomb, in which no one had ever been laid.
John 19:41

The Empty Tomb

Early on the first day of the week, while it was still dark, Mary
Magdalene went to the tomb and saw that the stone had been
removed from the entrance. So she came running to Simon Peter and
the other disciple, the one Jesus loved, and said, "They have taken the
Lord out of the tomb, and we don't know where they have put him!"

So Peter and the other disciple started for the tomb. Both were
running, but the other disciple outran Peter and reached the tomb
first. He bent over and looked in at the strips of linen lying there but
did not go in. Then Simon Peter, who was behind him, arrived and
went into the tomb. He saw the strips of linen lying there, as well
as the burial cloth that had been around Jesus' head. The cloth was
folded up by itself, separate from the linen. Finally the other disciple,
who had reached the tomb first, also went inside. He saw and
believed. (They still did not understand from Scripture that Jesus had
to rise from the dead.)

Jesus appears to Mary Magdalene

Then the disciples went back to their homes, but Mary stood outside
the tomb crying. As she wept, she bent over to look into the tomb
and saw two angels in white, seated where Jesus' body had been, one
at the head and the other at the foot. They asked her, "Woman, why
are you crying?"

"They have taken my Lord away," she said, "and I don't know where they have put him." At this, she turned round and saw Jesus standing there, but she did not realise that it was Jesus.

"Woman," he said, "why are you crying? Who is it you are looking for?"

Thinking he was the gardener, she said, "Sir, if you have carried him away, tell me where you have put him, and I will get him."

Jesus said to her, "Mary."

She turned towards him and cried out in Aramaic, "Rabboni!" (which means Teacher).

Jesus said, "Do not hold on to me, for I have not yet returned to the Father. Go instead to my brothers and tell them, 'I am returning to my Father and your Father, to my God and your God.'"

Mary Magdalene went to the disciples with the news: 'I have seen the Lord! And she told them that he had said these things to her.'

John 20:1-18

The Garden Tomb

At the place where Jesus was crucified,
there was a garden, and in the garden, a new tomb,
in which no one had ever been laid.
John 19:41

It was the first day of the week. Early morning. I like to think of the symbolism here: Jesus was laid in the tomb late in the day, as the Sabbath approached. The day was over and darkness was near. The Sabbath came and went and now a new day was beginning, and morning light was chasing away the darkness. A new era. A new testament. A new covenant. A new creation. A new self. A new heaven and earth.

In the east, on the edge of the horizon, there is a lightening in the dark, a thin band of the emerging sun. A lovely time of day. The light catches the smoke of early morning cooking fires rising above the flat roofs below. A cockerel crows announcing the day, heralding a different message from the one Peter heard last Friday morning.

People are waking, stretching, yawning; some are happy and eager for the day, others reluctant. For them, just another day. But not for Mary. She'd had a rough time. She loved Jesus passionately. When she first met him, he had accepted her without conditions, loving her as she was. And that love had re-oriented her life, made her whole. She had responded with love and faithfulness. The other disciples, the men, blew hot and cold. They misunderstood Jesus so often, quarrelling about their place in his Kingdom. Some had run away, but she had been constant, by his side.

Jean Vanier, who established L'Arche Community, says Mary was 'Glued to his side'. She was there at the cross, watching Jesus die. She felt his agony. I cannot imagine the pain that rooted her there by the cross: waiting, praying and weeping for him in spite of her own agony. She could not leave him. She watched, heartbroken, as the disciples took his broken body from the cross. She followed the despairing group as they stumbled their way to that unused tomb in the garden. All through Saturday, the Sabbath, she felt the numbness, the denial, and then the slow, weary acceptance of the tragedy.

Jesus, her friend, was dead.

Meditation

Oh how she wept.
Heart breaking,
eyes so full she could not see.
The face she loved so dearly,
lost
to the long dark night.
He who had restored her hope,
he who had brought her back to life
now lay
lifeless
on cold hard stone.
Alone.

Once so free,
spirit fearless,
joyful and immortal,
now bound in man-made shroud,
now blood-stained,
now mortally wounded.

Desolation.
She waits for dawn.

Prayer

Lord,
when all is dark,
and I am lost,
when hope lies amongst the rubble
of my life,
help me to wait.
For I know you will come.

Lord,
when the flow of my tears
washes away all understanding,
exposing deep wounds in my heart,
tell me to wait.
For I know you will come.

Lord,
when circumstances bind
and restrict the way ahead,
when the door is blocked and there
is no way out,
be with me as I wait.

For I know you will come
to roll away the stone.

A New Day

Early on the first day of the week...
John 20:1

It was a long night, a restless and fitful sleep. And then the coming of the dawn, bringing a relief of sorts. The relief of activity.

I can hear Mary saying, "It's all over. He's dead but now there are things to do." Sometimes it is all we can do; busying ourselves by picking up the threads of a frayed life. A way of coping with the unspeakable. She and the other women gather the spices together, no-one speaks, and moving as one, they go to the tomb. Did they dread going back, to face the finality of his death? Wondering who would move the stone so they could anoint his body?

Like a film in slow motion, with an atmosphere of overwhelming sadness, they move through the olive trees, voices hushed, intent on their purpose. Their shadows blending with the retreating night.

And then, suddenly, it's as if the film speeds up. The details vary – eyewitness accounts often do as people repeat their version of what happened. The women get to the tomb. They see the stone pushed aside, the tomb open. No stone, no guards, no body.

Mary rushes back to Peter. It's interesting that she goes to Peter first. He's still seen as leader, in spite of his denials. The scene offers our imagination a picture of opposites – the constant and the inconstant together. Mary and Peter. I think Peter goes with Mary to find John – I wonder why they weren't together? They had all scattered when Jesus was arrested but hadn't they got together later? Surely they needed each other more than ever at this point. But now the two of them, Peter and John, run to the tomb, with Mary following.

By the time Mary gets there, Peter and John have seen, and believed, and gone. Mary is left alone.

Prayer

Lord, Mary inspires me.
She had courage,
facing the hardest time of her life.
The brutal and unbearable loss
of the One who had saved her.
Lord, give me courage.

Lord, she must have dreaded
going back,
forced once more to admit
that you were gone.
Unwilling to see
the immensity of stone
blocking her way
to anoint your broken body.
Lord, let me see beyond the bounds
of possibility.

She must have wondered
who would move the stone away,
so she could offer the spices
and fill the stagnant air with
fragrance.

But the stone was gone.
And the grave was empty.

Hallelujah.

Meditation

Mary Magdalene.

Did Mary ever garden?
Dig the cold earth,
Sow seeds into damp darkness.
And wait?

Did she take cuttings?
And slant them, plant them like
crosses?
Then watch for life
Budding from dead wood?

And in the garden,
in the morning light,
when hope was dead and dry,
was the stone of grief
rolled away
in sudden blossoming?

Eddie Askew, Easter 2000

Who are you looking for?

... but Mary stood outside the tomb crying.
John 20:11

S he stands outside weeping, but why does she stay? She went to care for the body but it's gone so there's no use staying on. Except that she can't leave. She stays because that's where he was, where they left him, their hearts breaking as they laid him down on the cold and silent stone. She wants to be near, or at least to find out where he's been taken.

Through her tears she looks again into the tomb. 'Two angels in white, seated where Jesus's body had been, one at the head and the other at the foot'. They ask "Woman, why are you crying?" She answers with the words we know so well, "They've taken away my Lord, and I don't know where they have put him." I wonder who she thought 'they' were. The authorities?

Then there's a sudden movement. She turns. Her head is bowed, she doesn't look up. Through her tears she sees feet. A man's feet. The gardener. That's my simple explanation of why she didn't recognise Jesus. John Barclay suggests she was looking at the tomb, not at Jesus. Looking back to the past, not to the future. The future without him was too painful to face. And now his body had gone. Maybe, too, she didn't recognise him because it's hard to believe what you assume is impossible.

"Why are you crying?" It's the second time she's been asked that, and now, "Who is it you are you looking for?" How did he know that she was looking for someone? She asks him to tell her where her Lord is so that she can 'get him'. Still she doesn't recognise him in the depth of her grief. Jesus comes to us in so many ways. He comes to meet us in our distress and pain, our weakness and doubt. He came to Thomas later in the story. Thomas who declared he could not, would not, believe until he had seen and touched the risen Christ. Jesus met his need.

Often, Jesus comes in ways and through people we don't recognise – to strengthen, encourage and challenge. "Why are you crying?" These were the first words of the risen Christ. The first words of new life. She's the first person to hear him speak. Why to her? Was it simply because she'd put herself into a position where she could? Peter and John had rushed off. (If we want to hear God, do we need to create conditions where we can hear him?) Or was there a deeper reason? Was there part of her that still hoped for a miracle, a part that remembered his words promising life eternal, that spoke of his return? We can only wonder. It was a simple question, but for us there are reverberations on a massive scale. Why should we cry? Jesus is alive, his love released to the world. We know the full story. He is alive, and we are resurrection people, not Good Friday people.

Meditation

Alone she stood,
her world in pieces
at the foot of your cross.
Her hopes,
which you had renewed,
now lost
in an agony of grief.

She felt she understood.
She knew your heart,
or so she thought,
but never,
never
could she imagine
this to be the end.

And so she waited
close to the place
where you'd been laid.
She waited
fearing that leaving the garden
meant finally losing you.

She waited
for understanding to come.
She waited for you.

And then she heard your voice,
the sound came,
heralding her understanding.

Prayer

Lord, I choose to believe
that you are with me,
when circumstance tells me otherwise.

Lord, I choose to believe
that when understanding fails me
I can trust you.

Lord, I choose to believe
when friends fall away
and I am alone,
you are there.

Lord, I choose to believe
the simpler truth,
the greater truth,
that you are
who you say you are.

Lord, I choose you,
for I know
you have chosen me.

God calls us by name

Jesus said to her, "Mary."
John 20:16

Then he calls her by name. "Mary." Standing outside the empty tomb in the early morning light, she realises who this figure is and reaches out to him. Strange though it was, she didn't recognise him till then. Perhaps, the resurrected Christ was physically different.

He called her by name. Here are echoes of Isaiah's words, 'Fear not, for I have redeemed you; I have summoned you by name; you are mine' (*Isaiah 43:1*). He loves us with an everlasting and unconditional love which doesn't depend on our response. God loves his whole world as a package. God, in Jesus, loves his followers, his church, as a group. But he also loves every one of us as individuals. He loves Mary as Mary and calls her by name. And there is an instant recognition.

God loves because he is Love. He can do no other. God is all-powerful, but I believe that God can't not love. Love is the essence of his nature.

Mary reaches out to him, arms wide, grasping him. A natural reaction. Go to any airport and watch how people greet each other. The film *Love Actually* finishes with several very moving minutes of film taken at one of our major airports, which draws you in to the warmth and love of people being reunited. Wonderful to see. It's human to touch, hug, hold and kiss. Mary hopes and expects Jesus to reach out to her as he'd always done in the past. She'd seen him do it to so many. The paralysed man, the blind, the leprosy sufferer, the unwanted.

But not now. "Do not hold on to me." It must have hurt. It must have been hard not to feel it as a rejection. Mary had been so close to Jesus, so dependent on him. From the time they had first met he had transformed her life. After the agony of the cross, she has the heart-stopping joy of seeing him alive again, and now she wants to go back to where they were before. But that can't be. It's not possible. We can never go back in that sense. Everything is different.

Mary has to learn, as we all have to learn, that we can't simply hold onto the Jesus we first knew. Jesus is asking her to grow up into a new relationship with him. She had been so dependent, following him and doing what she was told. The decisions were made for her. Now she has to move on towards maturity.

The process of growing into maturity asks us to loosen our grip on what we know and hold on to so tightly, and to reach out into the unknown. To think for ourselves and make our own decisions. He'll still be there, but in a new way. Mary has to learn to hold on to the risen Lord, not in the old physical way, but to open her life so that he can live within her – and within us. A new, more mystical, but closer relationship than anything before.

Saint Augustine said, "God is closer to us than we are to ourselves." Jesus says that he will dwell within us, as the Father dwells in him. (Perhaps we don't hold on to him because he is already holding on to us.)

It's the same for all of us. Faith is about change. God wants us to grow and the only way to grow is to loosen our grasp on what we think we know so that we can deepen our understanding. This loosening isn't to deny our earlier experience, but it is to open ourselves to the possibility of reaching deeper levels of truth. God doesn't want us to stand still for fear of change, but to move on with him. It seems to me that sometimes it is easier to cling to the 'simple' truths of our early faith, finding the comfort of familiar ideas. If we cling on for fear of losing what we once knew, we are not free.

John tells us that 'Mary Magdalene went to the disciples with the news 'I have seen the Lord!' It was the first thing she did – shared the breathtaking news that she had seen Jesus. I can't help wondering if any of the others might have hoped to do this. Or were they all lost in the maelstrom of desperation and fear. Did anyone remember Lazarus, and allow a suspicion of hope to grow? Maybe this was not the end? That's all it takes, the mustard seed of faith and hope takes root.

Meditation

What did she feel
on hearing her name,
that voice so familiar,
heart leaping in recognition?

Reaching out to connect
with the resurrected Christ,
did she think all would be the same?
This body once broken
now stands restored,
together with her hope.

Alpha and Omega,
beginning and end,
her history transformed
and our story begun.

And so she runs,
from olive grove and angels
to a darkened upper room,
where fearful hearts behind heavy doors
wait for news
that will change their lives.

And they hear the words
'I have seen the Lord,
I have seen the Lord,'
crowding around her with hearts on fire,
a desperate love revived,
and a faith that will not fail.
Explosive power that rolled the stone away
now released to a waiting world.
Joy now rips through the temple curtain
spreading like fire from town to town.

He is alive.
He is alive.
Jesus is alive.

Prayer

Lord, it's easy to forget
the first joy of knowing you,
the longed for recognition
of when you first called me by name.

Understanding came easier then,
and sometimes I wish we were there still.
A simpler faith, and my questions seemed smaller.

Lord, help me to embrace the change
that leads to a deepening of faith,
releasing things which bind,
in exchange for your boundless freedom.

Freedom to love you,
with all of my heart,
my mind
and my strength.

Amen

A love that has no end

Go instead to my brothers and tell them...
John 20:17

Our God is an uncomfortable God, always inviting us to adventure, to break new ground in our faith. I have a problem with fundamentalist thought – wanting to preserve everything exactly as it is. Faithfulness is about following, travelling, not standing still. We fear losing what we already have, but only by loosening our grip on our understanding do we free ourselves enough to grow further in our faith.

R.S.Thomas, Welsh poet and clergyman, said, "He is such a fast God, always before us, and leaving as we arrive." There are times when Jesus seems far away, as if we have 'lost him'. Mary felt that at the empty tomb, asking, "Where have you taken him?" She is told, "Don't be afraid... He's not here." (*Mark 28:5*). She had not lost him, but all had changed, for her and for us. We have not lost him. He is simply ahead of us, calling us on by name.

I remember my grandchildren learning to ride bicycles. I can hear them shouting, "Don't let go! Hold me!" But we have to let go or they will never learn to ride. And when Jesus tells Mary to let go, he's not abandoning her but leading her into a new relationship. And what a relationship!

Read verse 17 again. 'Jesus said, "Do not hold on to me, for I have not yet returned to the Father. Go instead to my brothers and tell them, 'I am returning to my Father and your Father, to my God and your God.'" Through Jesus's death and resurrection, the special relationship he has with God is offered to her, to the disciples, to us.

"My Father your Father, My God your God," says Jesus. And here is the most incredible thing of all. The power and the love in which Jesus lived is ours. The power to live, to change, to grow. And to bring us to him. Do we really believe that? Do we dare to allow the immensity of that truth to penetrate every dimension of our lives? A power beyond our imagining. A love that has no end. This is the heart of our relationship with him. Endless possibility, endless love.

The Seeding

I do not know
who rolled the stone away
or how –
there is tale of angels
and of earthquakes,
but the process is irrelevant –
it matters only that the tomb
was empty
and that outside
the gardener
was seeding new life,
scattering it prodigally
into the waiting soil.

Eddie Askew

Prayer

The soil is ready, Lord
and we are the seed-bearers.
You tell us to go,
to scatter the seed wherever the soil.
A power beyond imagining,
your Spirit in us.

Lord, an endless gift,
that you need us
to carry new life.
Sowing in drought and in flood,
in harvest and in famine.
We are your image-bearers
for a hungry world,
with a family resemblance to the Divine.
Lord, give us strength to carry
your word with us wherever we go.

Six

The Eternal Garden

Reading: Revelation 21:1-4

Then I saw a new heaven and a new earth, for the first heaven
and the first earth had passed away. I saw the Holy City, the new
Jerusalem... and I heard a loud voice from the throne saying,
"Now the dwelling of God is with men, and he will live with them.
They will be his people, and God himself will be with them and be
their God. He will wipe away every tear from their eyes.
There will be no more death or mourning or crying or pain,
for the old order of things has passed away.

And so the story of the garden is complete – as complete as it can be in
our world today. In our deepest being, we still hold memories of the first
garden, Eden, of that pure open relationship between God and humanity. We
still feel a deep yearning for a closer relationship than we now have.

And isn't it that yearning that keeps drawing us on to search for more of him,
to see his handprint in our lives, to hear him calling us by name?

In Isaiah chapter 58 verse 11 we read: 'The LORD will guide you always; he
will satisfy your needs in a sun-scorched land and will strengthen your frame.
You will be like a well-watered garden, like a spring whose waters never fail.'

Not only are we looking for a return to the Garden of Eden, but God says
our lives are to be like a well-watered garden in themselves. An inner place of
rest and deep connection with him who made us. A place where in spite of
outward drought, we can be watered from within.

Jeremiah puts it this way in chapter 31 verse 12. 'They will come home and
sing songs of joy on the heights of Jerusalem. They will be radiant because of
the LORD's good gifts...Their life will be like a watered garden, and all their
sorrows will be gone' (*New Living Translation*).

Sometimes the Garden seems so far away, so remote a possibility. Yet there are times when what I call moments of transcendence break through into our world, when a feeling of the very real and undeniable presence of God suddenly overwhelms. Last winter, at 11pm, I was walking the dog under a cold but clear sky. I stood still under the brilliance of the stars and the whole earth seemed to expand. I felt a great sense of wonder. My smallness was caught up in the immensity of God and his universe. I had no words. They were not needed. It lasted a few seconds but I have carried it with me ever since then.

And yet there is another garden, the one promised to us at the end of our lives, the Garden of God spoken about in Revelation chapter 2 verse 7: 'To him who overcomes I will grant to eat from the tree of life, which is in the paradise of God.'

Some translations say 'in the garden of God', a true paradise with the River of Life running through it, and at its centre, the Tree of Life. Echoes of Eden again, but this time there will be no fall from grace. There will be no more tears, and no shame. No banishment from God's presence. No laboured life which ends in death. His reward to us is to enjoy his presence forever. In Genesis chapter 2, we read how: 'A river watering the garden flowed from Eden...' and now in Revelation chapter 22 verses 1–2 we learn about: 'the river of the water of life, as clear as crystal, flowing from the throne of God and of the Lamb... On each side of the river stood the tree of life... And the leaves of the tree are for the healing of the nations.'

The circle is complete. The story of God's unending love to us through the ages has been fulfilled.

And now the gate to the Garden is open again. The stone is rolled away and the road to new life is ahead. If stones do block our way, they can be removed. Stones of guilt and doubt, of fear and shame, of hesitation. All that hinders our communion with God can be removed. The stone of exile is rolled away. New life explodes from the open tomb like champagne from a shaken bottle. And Jesus, our loving Jesus, stands at the garden gate to welcome us back to the place we should never have left.

Meditation

One Glorious Day

One day,
one glorious day,
all
and all
and all will be well.

That which was lost
restored.
That which was broken
made new.

Love
that holds the cosmos
in its hand
will wipe away every tear.

Love
that called Lazarus
to life
from the cold, cold tomb,
will lead us
to life
eternal.

Beauty of Eden,
ours once more.
Heaven
with Earth restored.

The gate has been flung wide.
The King of Glory stands
to beckon us in.

Prayer

Lord,
whatever our story,
wherever we find ourselves today,
let us remember your story.
Your Son,
sent for love of us.
Your Son,
given for the rescue of all.

Let us remember
that this life leads to the next,
true and eternal,
a home with you.
Eden restored,
the earth redeemed,
and we are truly home,
with you.